ESSENTIAL TOOLS FOR
OPERATIONS
MANAGEMENT

ESSENTIAL

TOOLS FOR

OPERATIONS

MANAGEMENT

Tools, Models and Approaches for Managers and Consultants

Simon A. Burtonshaw-Gunn

A John Wiley & Sons, Ltd., Publication

This edition first published 2010
© 2010 Simon Burtonshaw-Gunn

Registered office
John Wiley & Sons Ltd, The Atrium, Southern Gate, Chichester, West Sussex,
PO19 8SQ, United Kingdom

For details of our global editorial offices, for customer services and for information
about how to apply for permission to reuse the copyright material in this book
please see our website at www.wiley.com.

The right of the author to be identified as the author of this work has been
asserted in accordance with the Copyright, Designs and Patents Act 1988.

A catalogue record for this book is available from the British Library.

ISBN 978-0-470-74592-2

Set in 11.5/15pt Bembo by Toppan Best-set Premedia Limited
Printed in Great Britain by TJ International Ltd, Padstow, Cornwall, UK

CONTENTS

ACKNOWLEDGEMENTS

From the feedback since the publication of my book *The Essential Management Toolbox* I have been asked to expand on the models and tools in a practical way; for me the value of the Toolbox book is to have a collection of tools which may be used for a variety of management assignments. Again in compiling this book I have to say that this would not have been possible without the fine efforts from all those management authors, research publications and course notes, etc. that I have collected over the years. As such I am greatly indebted to all whose work appears in the book, and also to my own teachers and mentors who have aided my own journey through many management topics.

I am very grateful to the publishers, individuals and copyright holders who gave their permission to allow previously published work to be used in this book and whilst every effort has been made to ascertain copyright and seek permission I apologize in advance for any omissions and would be pleased to correct these in any future edition.

Once again I am indebted to my friends at John Wiley and Sons for their support and encouragement. My sincere thanks also go to my friend, former colleague and regular academic writing partner, Dr Malik Salameh, for his significant input and support in this project, in providing constructive comments on my draft manuscripts and his willingness to pen a few words to set the scene for the reader.

FOREWORD

By Dr Malik Salameh

The importance of operations management as a core
business discipline as addressed by Professor Simon
Burtonshaw-Gunn, in this, his third book in the series
of *Essential Management* publications, will be familiar to
experienced leaders and managers – yet still succeeds in
contributing more value by helping identify potential
gaps in the operational delivery of prospective and established enterprises.

Once again the same effective formula has been main-
tained by providing a specialist focus on the area of business operations management; whilst recognizing the
importance of sharing this knowledge in a flexible format
– to satisfy the full range of business stakeholder needs;
and ensuring direct relevance to any size of business and
at any point in the business, product or service lifecycle.

A regular feature of the *Essential Tool* series is the way
they strike a subtle balance in reinforcing the essential
hard points for an established business, its employees and
strategic management – whilst offering the opportunity

to ensure hidden norms are challenged appropriately and informed business improvement options are developed. A key feature of this book is the range of example business plan formats included, enabling the reader to tailor them easily to suit their specific environment – either as an "acid test" in the realization of innovative ideas or in supporting projects to secure the necessary funding.

Furthermore, for the start-up business or those new to the corporate arena, it offers a comprehensive review of the fundamentals of operations management and an expert accompanying narrative, which constructively scrutinizes business propositions. It carefully marries a range of management tools and techniques to provide a comprehensive response to the key organizational and environmental scenarios likely to be faced by any business or individual.

A differentiating value of this publication lies in its ability to help fulfil the often unforeseen requirements to conduct urgent functional or organizational audits in response to changes in external or internal market or regulatory dynamics. Therefore building on the theme of self-managed learning, the operations management content is presented in such away as to enable any user to take the frameworks and associated guidance to conduct an intermediate level audit in a confident and informed manner, and within a fairly short lead time.

I strongly recommend this book as an invaluable source of such transferable knowledge and for the clarity it provides in the field of operations management.

BIOGRAPHICAL DETAILS

Professor Simon A. Burtonshaw-Gunn has over 30 years' working experience with a technical background in mechanical and nuclear engineering, research and development and on-site major plant commissioning followed by over 12 years in project management in both technical consultancy and hardware projects for the UK Ministry of Defence. He joined British Aerospace in 1994 (now BAE Systems) undertaking project management of specialist consultancy work within Russia, Ukraine and Belarus. He has held the post of Head of Project Management before being appointed as a managing consultant leading a consultancy team undertaking assignments including business strategy planning, change management, organizational development and management training covering a range of organizations and industries. As a practising management consultant he has undertaken assignments in over 20 countries in Asia, North Africa, the Middle and Far East and Eastern Europe and currently is a principal management consultant for an international management consultancy company based in the UK working in both the public and private sectors. To complement this experience he holds two Master's degrees and a PhD in various strategic management topics together with fellowship of four professional bodies including the Chartered Management Institute (FCMI) and the Institute of Business Consulting (FIBC). In 2009 he was appointed as one of the first Goodwill Ambassadors for the Chartered Management Institute.

He was a post-doctoral research fellow for four years at the Manchester Metropolitan University before relinquishing this at the beginning of 2005 to take up the role of a visiting professor at the University of Salford in Greater Manchester. Here he served for three years in the six-star research rated School of the Built Environment before being appointed as the first visiting professor to the Salford Business School in 2007. In addition, he held a two-year appointment as a member of the Court at the University of Leeds – a member of the Russell Group association of the top 20 UK research-intensive universities – until mid 2009.

Professor Burtonshaw-Gunn has been a research examiner for the UK's Chartered Institute of Purchasing and Supply (CIPS) since 2002 and is one of the founding members of an international academic research group (ISCRiM) with a focus on supply chain risk management. In connection with this group he has presented conference papers in Sweden, the USA, UK and Hungary together with a number of refereed publications, professional journal articles and chapters in four collaborative management textbooks. On the subject of risk management, last year he published a book covering "Risk and Financial Management in Construction" aimed at industry practitioners and post-graduate students. His popular book *The Essential Management Toolbox* covering management tools, models and notes aimed at students, managers and consultants was published by John Wiley and Sons in 2008.

INTRODUCTION

This book has been driven from an interest in the use of management tools and models published in January 2008 in *The Essential Management Toolbox: Tools, Models and Notes for Managers and Consultants*. This supplementary book describes a number of examples and shares the author's practical experience in deploying appropriate management tools and models taken from the Toolbox with a focus on operational management and its activities including related consultancy activities.

As an introduction this book comprises five broad and inter-related chapters to the extent that each is a natural progression from the subsequent chapter and yet these too influence the earlier steps. It commences with an examination of the major management topics of strategy, quality and business continuity; all necessary for business performance. The second chapter on business planning reflects company capabilities, vision and strategic objectives; and whilst there will be some specific features to each organization, a number of example business plans are presented to assist in this process. This leads to Chapter 3 which explores the topic of product development although this should also be influenced by market research and an understanding of customer requirements. Chapter 4 looks at supply chain management which is a growing feature of business as witnessed by the increasing use of global suppliers and the use of collaborative working. The final chapter, Chapter 5, concentrates on the role of people management as both individuals and in managing teamwork.

Each of the topics of these chapters has been chosen to provide a logical framework to these inter-related management topics within operations management commencing at the strategic level of the organization and moving through to present a tactical focus from managing suppliers and the organization's own staff, as shown in Figure I.1.

Whilst the intent has been to provide an opportunity to discuss some new models, the majority of the figures and models are taken from *The Essential Management Toolbox: Tools, Models and Notes for Managers and Consultants* published by John Wiley and Sons in 2008. Where the original source is not the author's then the source is shown with each model discussed.

The book is designed to be one of a series of sibling publications intended to group enabling management tools, techniques and models into related clusters giving students and practitioners a highly effective means of

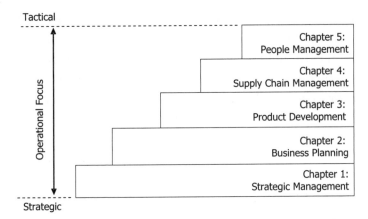

Figure I.1 Framework for the book rationale.

developing both at an individual level and organization-ally. The intent of writing this title has been to provide a suitable platform to understand and undertake practical performance improvements with an equal relevance whether within the public or private sectors. Previous titles in the series are *Essential Tools for Organizational Performance* applicable across a range of businesses and users and *Essential Tools for Management Consulting* with a focus more on providing suitable management tools to practising consultants and their clients.

The structure follows the successful "The Essential Management Toolbox" formula of integrating contem-porary management tools, techniques and models with those developed from practical experience of addressing the challenges of management consulting across multiple industries. As with *The Essential Management Toolbox* and the other books in this series the references provided guide the reader to where further information may be found. In addition, each chapter is punctuated by key theme subheadings to aid navigation and provide a logical approach to each topic area.

CHAPTER 1

STRATEGIC MANAGEMENT

INTRODUCTION

Many works on strategic management treat the subject as consisting of several component parts such as goal formulation, strategic evaluation, strategy implementation and strategic control, but advise that these are components of a framework and may not exist as discrete orderly steps in a strategic management decision-making process. It is further suggested that there are a number of characteristics of strategic decision making concerned with the scope of an organization's activities, the matching of the organization to the environment and then matching the organization's activities to its resource capability.

Within this first chapter there are a number of well-known business models, many of which help to achieve a comprehensive analysis of the business in order to determine its future direction, or at least make decisions based on informed choice and then plan how this can be best deployed or realized. In addition, the words "strategy" and "strategic management" relate to a number of levels within an organization and a hierarchy of these together with inter-related strategies is shown in this section (see Figure 1.1). The lowest level of strategy is

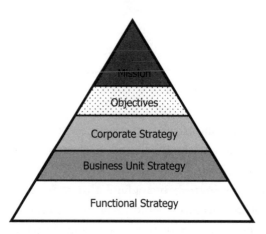

Figure 1.1 Hierarchy of strategies.
From *The Essential Management Toolbox: Tools, Models and Notes for Managers and Consultants*, S.A. Burtonshaw-Gunn, 2008. Reproduced with permission.

often referred to as "Functional strategy" which focuses on the day-to-day operational activities that the organization is involved in. Within a business there are often a number of functional strategies which take their lead from the next level of "Business strategy". This intermediate level business strategy covers the aggregation of the functional strategies for a single business unit or organization with a concentration on the tactics that the business will use to address its threats from competitors and market opportunities with present or targeted customers. The business strategy should reflect the higher level "Corporate strategy". This highest strategy level needs to consider the overarching strategy of the business to address questions concerning the arena in which the business should compete and how the organization's activities contribute to its competitive advantage and longer-term sustainability. It should also reflect the organization's mission, vision and objectives seen in its business plan and covered in detail in Chapter 2.

Whilst there are many books on strategic or corporate management with a natural focus on long-term organizational development, this chapter examines strategic management from the context of operations management and how these two topics can coexist. The strategic "big picture" decisions should not just be about the commercial performance of the business, as they should also include the commitment and development of its operational performance; none more so than with quality, environmental and business continuity management – as these three become more closely aligned through common external standards and interoperability of customer requirements. This first chapter, then, examines how corporate strategy is established, its role and benefits as a prelude to the other chapters and then explores the areas of business operations management.

STRATEGY AND PERFORMANCE DRIVERS

It is useful to remember that within both commerce and industry the *raison d'être* for the senior level of management, normally the executive board of directors, is to examine the nature of the business and steer the company to its future sustainability. Such direction requires the establishment and implementation of a robust strategy, which will be primarily concerned with the company as a whole, its environment and its future course. Indeed, such strategy formulation will inevitably have to draw on an analysis of its present business role, the future business direction it wishes to take and how the board's vision and objectives can be successfully implemented and achieved. It has to be said that strategic management is a general term, whereas the above decisions regarding what business to be in are generally covered under the term "corporate strategy". This task of strategy development involves decisions on plans at the most senior level which recognize both the financial and organizational

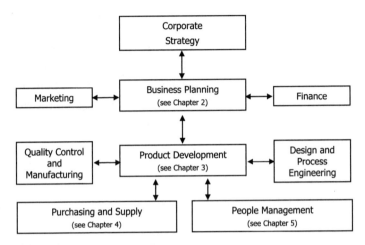

Figure 1.2 Strategy integration.

development of the company with such major decision making regarded as being at the very heart of this branch of management. However, development of a corporate strategy should not be regarded as an isolated task limited to a few but rather it must be integrated with other key corporate or stakeholder functions, as shown in Figure 1.2. As seen, the model also provides a natural linkage to the other topics within this book.

The model in Figure 1.2 demonstrates the importance of the relationship between corporate strategy and business strategy. This must then be articulated in integrated business plans to envision how the organization will engage in its business activities and in turn how these drive the functional strategies such as product development which details the value-adding work that the organization undertakes.

Strategic management involves not just trying to exploit the strengths of the organization and minimize any weaknesses, but requires that the organization also considers the external environment in which it operates, typically looking for opportunities and threats which it may have to respond to. The strategic perspective goes beyond operational efficiency improvements as the development of an effective strategy will need to focus on delivering and maintaining distinctive quality products, high customer and brand awareness and trust, and must also be seen to support overall business growth targets. In general terms the development of a strategy, whether for a newly established or a mature organization, will involve addressing the following four key areas:

- **Analysis** of strategic goals (vision, mission and strategic objectives) along with the analysis of the internal and external environment of the organization.
- **Decision making** on the key areas of organizational development and the most effective ways to address them.
- **Implementation** by identifying and deploying resources, structures and systems to implement the strategy efficiently and effectively.
- **Support** from the provision and maintenance of policies, organizational infrastructure, governance, culture and leadership which all play a role in supporting strategy implementation.

To achieve any degree of success many writers on the topic of strategic management stress that the organization's corporate vision must be aligned to its core values; to the organization's mission; and also to its goals and the objectives it wishes to pursue in the short, medium and long term. In general, it is also recognized that the absolute prime importance to any company, irrespective of its size or its public/private ownership state, must be its desire to survive over the long term. This may be achieved by balancing the need to earn an economic profit (and satisfy its shareholders) with the need to invest in its own resources; typically its systems, processes, plant, machinery or its employees. The efficient use of these "human resources" largely governs the success of the organization as it is ultimately reliant on its employees to both formulate and implement strategy. Strategic management may therefore involve the development, review and remoulding of the organizational structure that will best ensure survival within its operating environment, taking into account the internal and external pressures which currently impact or have the potential to impact business operations, as shown in the model of Figure 1.3.

The analysis stage should be fully integrated with wider competitor knowledge and how this will influence the business operation of the organization. The simple Strengths, Weaknesses, Opprtunities and Threats (SWOT) analysis is often a good starting point in exploring the internal and external influences which can then be further

- Potential reduction in staff
- Moratorium on new recruitment
- Reduction in skills and knowledge and/or loss of process knowledge
- Squeeze on current spending and planned budget reductions
- Staff training and development seen as discretionary
- Ability to maintain standards of service quality and quality assurance systems
- Increased pressure on staff performance with corresponding increase in risk of accidents

- Shareholders' expectations
- Reduction in suppliers
- Reduction in customer base
- Increased operating costs
- Need to maintain business reputation
- Need to protect brand
- Additional resources needed on supply chain issues
- Need to adhere to legislative requirements
- Needs to maintain health, safety and environmental standards

Figure 1.3   Business pressures influencing strategy.

refined with other tools and models such as those described below.

1. The Ansoff Matrix

This covers the relationship between market and product and suggests four possible strategies which the business may adopt for each product or service (Figure 1.4). This widely applicable matrix can be used to provide guidance for companies in setting their strategic objectives or for analysis to understand their current market position. It examines choices based on the relationship between the organization's products and their market position and is usually undertaken for each product or service within the company's portfolio. Understanding this position offers some direction to future strategy.

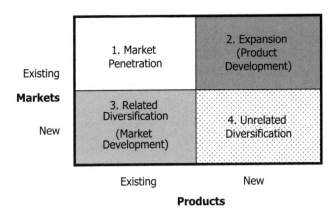

Figure 1.4 Product–market growth strategies.
Reprinted by permission of *Harvard Business Review*. An exhibit from "Strategies for diversification" by H. Igor Ansoff, Sept.–Oct. 1957. Copyright by the President and Fellows of Harvard College. All rights reserved.

2. Porter's Generic Strategies

Professor Michael Porter sugests that three generic strategies can be adopted, these are:

- Cost leadership.
- Differentiation.
- Focus.

The simplest of the above strategies is **cost leadership** and by achieving the lowest cost of production in an industry or market sector, a company can either reduce its selling prices or keep the increased profits to invest in research and develop new and more of existing products. The second option of **differentiation** involves making the product or service appear different in the mind of the consumer, this may be by offering better design, reliablity, service and delivery; for services this may include courtesy, availability, expertise and location. The third strategy of **focus** is where a company concentrates on a market area, or to deliver niche products or services.

3. "Five forces model"

Professor Porter's "Five forces model" can be used as part of the organization's strategy planning process and also to ensure that the actions (current or proposed) are aligned with its strategy and its market position aspirations. The use of the model can help to identify where additional information may be required to assist the company in its strategy development with suggestions for future competitive strategies. Porter's model covers:

- the bargaining power of suppliers and buyers;
- the threats from subsitutes and new entrants; and
- the intensity of rivalry among competitors.

This model is shown also in *Essential Tools for Management Consulting* as it provides a good structure to consider the "big picture" external perspectives.

4. Elements of Corporate Strategy

This model is the main proposition for strategic management shown in the textbook *Exploring Corporate Strategy* by Professors Gerry Johnson and Kevan Scholes. This summary model of the strategic management process concerns three major elements: strategic analysis; strategic choice; and strategic implementation with each having its own inter-related subsets of supporting considerations/actions (Figure 1.5). Each of these inter-related elements is crucial in defining and succeeding in establishing a robust strategy to take an organization forward. The supporting parts of Strategic Analysis identify the company circumstances. The topics with Strategic Choice will prompt an assessment of the suitability and rationale based on strategic logic, research evidence and cultural fit. Finally, the Strategic Implementation elements need to be considered and addressed in translating the selected strategy into action.

5. Portfolio Strategies

There are a number of approaches available; however, the most widely used is that from the Boston Consulting Group which, through a matrix model, provides guidance on current and future market positions and how these may be managed. This is shown as Figure 1.6.

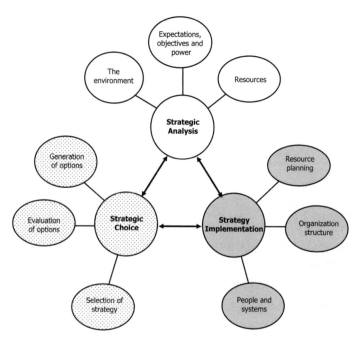

Figure 1.5 Elements of corporate strategy.
From Professor Gerry Johnson and Professor Kevan Scholes, *Exploring Corporate Strategy*, 2002, 6th edition text and cases. Reproduced with permission of Pearson Publishing.

The BCG model matches high and low industry growth with the company's high and low relative market share. From this model four main categories are then established relative to the product and its performance:

- The Star is a high–market share business in a high-growth industry, providing high cash flow but requir-

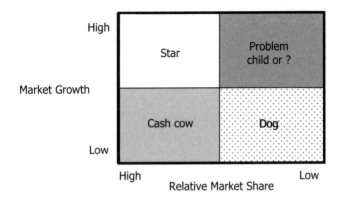

Figure 1.6   Product performance matrix.
The BCG Portfolio Matrix reproduced with kind permission of the Boston Consulting Group. Copyright © 1970. All rights reserved.

ing high levels of funding. Star products or services grow and finance themselves.

- The Question mark – high industry growth with low relative market share, providing low cash generation but needing high levels of funding. These are also referred to as "problem children" because of the amount of time that is required and that they need funding to grow. If they become successful they become "stars" or "cash cows".

- The Cash cow is a high-market share business in a low-growth industry, providing large positive cash flow with low levels of funding.

- The Dog is a small market share business in a low-growth industry providing positive or negative cash flow. These businesses are at the end of the product lifecycle and need a face lift or to be phased out if going nowhere; they also consume corporate funds and management time in an attempt to stay competitive.

It has to be said that portfolio strategies have their drawbacks as they do not take into account the linkages between products (or services); it has to be remembered that many organizations share technical, marketing and support functions and the costs of these may often be amortized across all products; they may also be difficult to apportion from a business reporting performance perspective. In addition, some products or services may be offered as non-earning, private venture, development projects requiring investment with no identified reward.

Having analysed the organization and its business environment, and concluded by making appropriate decisions, the next stage is in strategy implementation. Whilst this implementation may be a continuation of established strategic plans it may also necessitate an organizational change. Strategy implementation will need to recognize the level of difficulty of introducing change and the model shown as Figure 1.7 shows a range of change options which an organization may need to adopt. The model also suggests that the easier changes at the bottom of the pyramid offer the least level of discomfort for, and resistance from, employees and that these lower level changes also require the least amount of time and cost. Similarly, the higher levels necessitate substantial time and

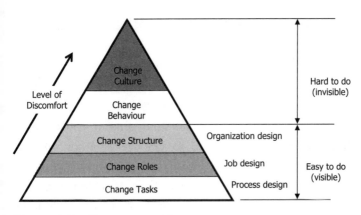

Figure 1.7 Change pyramid.
From *The Essential Management Toolbox: Tools, Models and Notes for Managers and Consultants*, S.A. Burtonshaw-Gunn, 2008. Reproduced with permission.

investment and as such are generally more difficult to implement. The pyramid model also suggests that embarking on the lower level changes first may be a good way to develop involvement and an acceptance to a change programme especially if quick, beneficial and easy to observe changes can be realized by this staged approach – a clear example of harvesting "the low hanging fruit" first.

After considering the above factors it is proposed that there will be a number of approaches which can be deployed in change implementation. (The subject of change management is covered in greater detail in the *Essential Tools for Organizational Performance*, also published by John Wiley and Sons.)

STRATEGIC PERFORMANCE TOOLS

Having spent time, effort and no doubt money on the activities associated with strategy analysis, identification and development, this chapter now looks at some of the other "big picture" strategic management tools which have become widely used in practice in large international organizations and are increasingly being considered in other businesses. The first of these is quality – a term not to be confused with "luxury". In this sense quality relates to the product or service provided meeting customer requirements, its suitability or fitness for purpose, how the product provides customer satisfaction and finally questioning if the product or service provides value for money in terms of quality and price. This approach is sometimes called total quality management (TQM) or just TQ or QM depending on the company. Some 50 years ago the focus was on quality control with an emphasis on inspection and reducing scrap; this moved to quality assurance in the 1970s with a concentration on working to systems and procedures to help maintain consistency and conformance; finally, since the 1980s there has been a move to TQM where people are responsible for the quality of their own work to a standard often set by the customer. Indeed, the focus here is on the results of the output.

At the same time as these advances there has been a shift to performance management and the measuring of key performance indicators as a predictive means of identifying deterioration of performance and helping to gain greater value from performance management by identifying areas of improvement. The management of performance in organizations typically covers:

- Linking corporate goals with department and/or individual performance.
- Identifying the key results areas.
- Identifying critical success factors.
- Clarifying key competences.

Widespread adoption of this approach has grown in number and has enabled companies to realize the benefits from sharing, in a non-competitive way, the working methods with other companies and from this the establishment of best practice and "benchmarking" has become commonplace since the 1990s. In support of all of the above was a move for formal external recognition of good practice and two quality frameworks are described below as examples of cross-industry sharing and commitment to continuous improvement.

The first of these is the US Quality Award which uses a point scoring framework to assess company performance as follows:

- Customer satisfaction 30%
- Leadership 10%
- Quality results 18%
- Information and analysis 7%
- Human resource utilization 15%

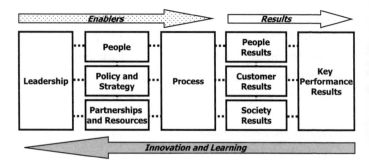

Figure 1.8   The EFQM Business Excellence Model.
Reproduced with thanks to the European Foundation of Quality
Management. Copyright © 1999–2003 EFQM.

- Strategic quality planning 6%
- Quality assurance systems 14%

This is known as the Malcolm Baldrige National
framework and is the forerunner to the second example,
the European Foundation for Quality Management's
(EFQM) Business Excellence Model, which since its
launch in 1989 has become the most widely used non-
prescriptive management model in Europe. Again, as in
the Baldrige framework, a similar scoring system is
employed but the linkages between the enabling functions and the business results are more obvious, as shown
in Figure 1.8. Each of the nine key areas is scored using
the following weighted scoring system:

- Leadership (10%): How the behaviours and actions
  of the executive team and all other leaders inspire,

support and promote excellence as the best way to achieve the organization's objectives.

- People management (9%): How the organization formulates, deploys, reviews and turns policy and strategy into plans and actions.
- Policy and strategy (8%): How the organization releases the full potential of its people.
- Resources (9%): How the organization manages resources effectively and efficiently.
- Processes (14%): How the organization manages, reviews and improves its processes.
- People satisfaction (9%): What the organization is achieving in relation to the satisfaction of its people.
- Customer satisfaction (20%): What the organization is achieving in relation to the satisfaction of its external customers.
- Impact on society (6%): The organization's impact on local, regional and national society.
- Business results (15%): What the organization is achieving in relation to its planned objectives and expectations of everyone with an interest or stake in the organization.

Although many companies have for a long time measured their strategic performance and the quality of their product or services, there has been less emphasis on the measurement of employee and customer satisfaction until the use of the above model. There is also a growing use of performance measures which are financial and non-

Performance indicator	Performance measure
Employee related	Employee satisfaction
	Attendance
	Turnover or "churn" including attrition rates, recruitment success, etc.
	Safety
	Suggestions
Operational	Reliability
	Delivery
	Processing times
	Lead times
	Inventory turnover (stock turn)
	Errors
	Costs of rework, etc.
Customer satisfaction	Overall index
	Retention
	Complaints
Market and financial	Market share
	Cash
	Profit
	Return on assets
	Return on stock
	Sales per employee

Figure 1.9   Identifying performance measures.

financial, internal and external, tangible and non-tangible and top-down and bottom-up. Figure 1.9 also supports the above quality models in linking performance to key business areas.

These performance measures can be used to show which of the strategic objectives are critical to the business, how the actual performance fits with the long-term business plans and what areas need to be addressed as a matter of urgency. However, it should be remembered that the customer will always be the true judge of performance, hence the emphasis on customer satisfaction scoring in the Baldrige and EFQM models.

Returning to the general topic of quality management, many companies work to prescribed systems not just to ensure their own business performance but also to demonstrate to potential customers that they are professionally managed with external accreditation to an acceptable and established recognized standard. The International Organization for Standardization is the world's largest developer and publisher of International Standards with a network across 159 countries based in its central headquarters in Geneva, Switzerland. This organization publishes the ISO9001-4 series of standards covering quality management which are also aligned with the similar management standard covering environmental management, ISO14001. This is the most widely used standard for environmental risk management and is closely aligned to the European Eco-Management and Audit Scheme (EMAS). Whilst the most basic reason for accepting environmental responsibility is to stay within the law, as environmental legislation becomes more stringent such conformance will affect an increasing number of companies' ability to deliver sustainable growth and even their survival. In addition, often "society" has increased expectations or demands, particularly on large companies. This is partly based on the perception that the larger organiza-

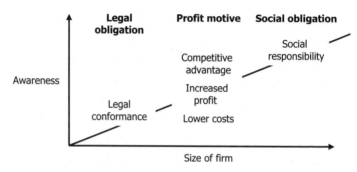

Figure 1.10   Environmental drivers.
Reproduced with kind permission of Kit Sadgrove, from *The Green Guide to Profitable Management*, Gower Publications, 1994.

tions should lead by example and that in proportion to their turnover or profit they are better able to afford the investment in meeting even tighter environmental requirements fulfilling a corporate responsible existence, as shown in Figure 1.10.

From a strategic perspective, one standard which has yet to be accepted with the same status as quality or environmental management is that covering business continuity management (BCM). This is a management process designed to provide a framework to ensure the resilience of an organization in any eventuality, with the aim of ensuring continuity of service to key customers and importantly protection of the company's brand and business reputation. As such BCM should be considered by small companies as well as larger corporations as the key five steps will be the same for all organizational sizes:

- Understand the vulnerabilities of the business.
- Define a business continuity strategy.
- Develop a plan.
- Undertake cultural change with appropriate training.
- Rehearse the plan.

Guidance for this strategic management topic can be seen in the British Standard 25999, rather than the ISO series; in addition, for those tasked with the development of their own organization's approach to BCM there are a number of websites sharing their approaches of BCM. BCM is gaining in use particularly in those critical national industries such as airlines, for example, especially where they also have public service obligations as one of their strategic drivers.

The final strategic performance tool of this chapter is the incorporation of strategic planning and objective setting with a recognition of the advantages of a knowledge economy, where business is supported by the intellectual property of its resources rather than its more reproducible operational products or services − a point also recognized by the difficulty in trying to identify an organization's unique selling proposition (USP) when compared to its competitors. It has to be said that over the years many companies have been trying to develop techniques to capture and share knowledge across their operations. In this regard organizations often view knowledge management as a relationship between people, technology, processes, strategy and a cultural context and on this basis usually consider that it requires inputs from human resources management, strategic management, organizational studies and IT systems. The initial challenge for many organizations eager to adopt knowledge management to stimulate innovation and growth has been in bringing these together to establish initially what they already know. Typically, the most easily accessible knowledge within any business is the "potential knowledge" in the form of raw data. However, the level of difficulty increases markedly for any business when attempting the acquisition of "tacit knowledge" and its accompanying synthesis by the organization's leadership population. This higher level of analysis relies heavily on the organization's ability to successfully convert tacit knowledge into explicit or transferable forms in a timely manner, which then can be shared across the business to contribute to the longer-term strategic direction of the business.

There are a number of strategies open to knowledge management for actively managing knowledge such as encouraging individuals to share their knowledge through a reciprocal knowledge sharing repository, such as a database, or allowing individuals to make knowledge requests to subject matter experts when specialist knowledge is required. Other knowledge management strategies for companies include:

- Cross-project learning.
- Project close-out and after-action reviews.

- Knowledge mapping of skills and topics by individuals.
- Establishing internal communities of practice.
- Best practice transfer, use of external benchmarking clubs.
- Introduction of competence management systems providing evaluation and planning of competences and succession planning for key organizational roles.
- Establishing a "master–apprentice" relationship providing coaching, mentoring and career support.
- Collaborative technologies and partnering arrangements.
- Performance measuring and reporting intellectual capital (a way of making explicit knowledge for companies).
- Social software such as social bookmarking, blogs, twitter, Web2, 2nd Life, etc.

Having mentioned that knowledge management may be considered as a strategic performance tool, it has to be said that for those embracing this it will also be a requirement to ensure that appropriate governance is in place to protect both the employee and the business – especially when considering the interaction between specialized knowledge and scarce skills. With competitive pressures on businesses which may include downsizing and undertaking major corporate change in the organization's strategic direction, it has also to be remembered that it is easy for valuable knowledge to be lost forever by such action. Of course, whilst there are normally advantages in such organizational changes this has to be balanced with the risk that such change will be undermined by corporate amnesia witnessed by examples across all businesses by spending hours on issues that previously took minutes. The final point also to recognize is that the loss of staff and valuable knowledge arises not only from the organization's actions but also with increased knowledge worker mobility. This can have a significant impact on the market capitalization of the business, thus impacting on shareholder value and eventually threatening its survival.

CHAPTER 2

BUSINESS PLANNING

INTRODUCTION

Without doubt it is safe to say that the task of business planning is applicable to all businesses whether as a sole trader or a multinational conglomerate. The production of a business plan is needed to describe the business, its objectives, its strategies, the market it is in and its financial forecasts. It is often used as a tool for measuring the performance of the organization against that intended over a short- or medium-term period, typically three to five years. For many new businesses the business plan may be used as a tool to promote an interest in the business and to secure external funding and as such needs to be undertaken as a serious task. At the outset the production of a business plan will help the organization to:

- Describe and explain its business idea or proposition.
- Provide a structure to the short- and longer-term plans.
- Uncover any problem areas that might be lurking.
- Identify unforeseen opportunities.
- Record the financial details.
- Provide an overview of the bigger picture.
- Provide an integrated framework for all of the business ideas.
- Make the business statistically more likely to succeed.
- Identify the risks that the business may face or prevent progress.

Another view is that a business plan is vital to:

- Gaining financial support from internal and external sources.
- Helping the organization to establish operating objectives and to measure results on a realistic basis.
- Helping to define a "road map" of where the company is now, where you want it to be, how and when it will get there, and at what cost.

This chapter commences by looking at the process of business planning, the production of a business plan and what it should cover. It then provides some example business plans which may be of help to those involved in this process and ends by proposing that a feasibility check is undertaken on the final plan. This checklist can be used to provide the organization with a degree of surety before sharing its plan with other parties. On completion of the task a checklist for the business plan feasibility covers the key questions of management, marketing and financial aspects of the plan which need to be addressed either directly or indirectly in the business plan.

BUSINESS PLANNING

It would be odd to find a company that did not undertake market research, look at its current performance, products and services and plan its future based on some meaningful objectives – if only to increase its customer satisfaction results and overall business performance. Without doubt each company will have a unique business plan applicable to its own objectives and aspirations; however, there are a number of common themes that each is likely to share. In addition, a business plan has several purposes, as it:

- Prompts management to examine logically the business in a structured way and consider what it currently does and what it wishes to do in the future.
- Encourages management to set future business objectives and then monitor progress against the plan.

- Identifies the resources and time needed to implement the business plan.
- Can be used to communicate the key features of the business plan to employees and stakeholders to provide them with an awareness of the business's direction.
- Provides links to the detailed, short-term functional strategies.

The basic stages in producing a business plan follows a logical planning cycle which also looks at past performance and what needs to be addressed as new targets and objectives are set. Indeed, the focus on the business plan is likely to be on three areas: establishing realistic goals for the business to aim for; demonstrating how its objectives will be met; and finally identifying what resources in terms of people, plant and investment will be required by the organization to achieve the realization of the new business plan.

The simple model of Figure 2.1 has links to research and data gathering, analysis and options studies; to strategic management in the form of setting objectives; and finally to performance management often related to people performance objectives.

Whilst this model is shown here in a business planning context it may also be used at an individual level as part of career appraisal and in personal development identification. This topic is also covered as part of Chapter 5: People Management. The questions in the model prompt some investigation into past performance and

Figure 2.1   The planning cycle.
From *The Essential Management Toolbox: Tools, Models and Notes for Managers and Consultants*, S.A. Burtonshaw-Gunn, 2008. Reproduced with permission.

what the organization may be expected to do in the future to improve performance. The model of Figure 2.2 is a natural development of this questioning approach and, together with establishing a view of the future for the organization, identifies barriers or constraints. This model can be linked to a workshop format to maximize on the amount of involvement, creative thinking and agreement to a way forward. In addition, this model also draws upon the SWOT (Strengths, Weaknesses, Opportunities and Threats) analysis tool and balances these features against the organization's longer-term goals

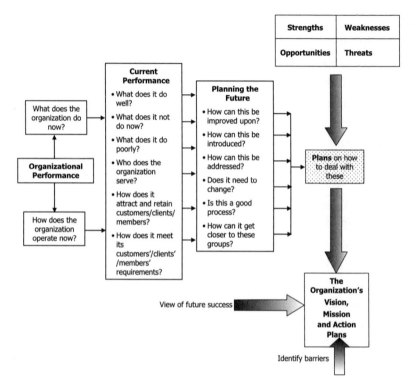

Figure 2.2   Understanding the product/service as part of the business planning process.
From *The Essential Management Toolbox: Tools, Models and Notes for Managers and Consultants*, S.A. Burtonshaw-Gunn, 2008. Reproduced with permission.

and its overall vision. The barriers to implementation can be identified at this stage; typically, these may be financial or a function of the external environment and thus are sometimes outside the direct control of the organization.

Often barriers are internal and can be managed through regular and open communications, good planning and appropriate management actions.

For new businesses whether product or service based, the business plan should also describe how the company will operate from its launch until it has established itself in the marketplace. In practice there should be a detailed narrative on the first six months of its trading as this is when costs in establishing the business are being incurred – in developing a market, recruiting staff, negotiating with suppliers, etc., contrasted with no or limited income, particularly if part of a supply chain when customers' terms of payment are unlikely to be favourable in timescale and hence the subject of cash flow needs to be understood and fully described.

The task of business planning should rest with one individual to act as the central point and main compiler although it will also benefit from wider participation with other senior managers and key departmental stakeholders; as such this task also lends itself to a facilitated "workshop" approach (for some guidance on workshops see also *Essential Tools for Management Consulting*). As shown in Figure 2.3 this model demonstrates the clear relationship between the external facing business strategy and the internally focused product strategy which is concerned with how the overall corporate strategy can be met by the business. This model also acknowledges the business management functions of finance, quality, human resource management, and marketing.

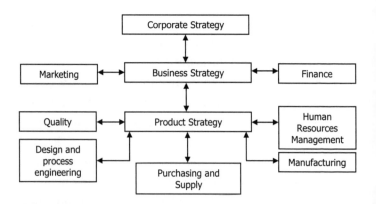

Figure 2.3   Inter-related strategies.
From *The Essential Management Toolbox: Tools, Models and Notes for Managers and Consultants*, S.A. Burtonshaw-Gunn, 2008. Reproduced with permission.

Whilst the first model of this chapter (Figure 2.1) showed a cyclical process, this should be regarded as only part of the overall process which in total should cover four main stages as shown in Figure 2.4 and described below.

Stage 1: Planning. As already mentioned, this first stage describes in written form the management's best estimate of future operations which is set out in a logical and organized way. Whilst some example business plans are provided later in this chapter, it should be noted that although there is no prescribed business plan format, adopting an established approach will often be useful in meeting investor expectations to show how the business is managed. This first stage should also crystallize ideas, and identify any risks or areas for further analysis. The business plan will describe in detail how the organization

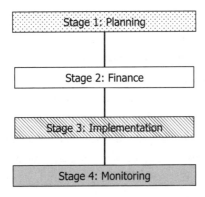

Figure 2.4   Stages of business planning.
From *The Essential Management Toolbox: Tools, Models and Notes for Managers and Consultants*, S.A. Burtonshaw-Gunn, 2008. Reproduced with permission.

will grow the business and over a longer-term reduce its reliance on external investors, such as banks, governments, private investors and so on. The business plan should discuss how it will develop and retain an increased market share and how much this will cost in marketing effort and promotion costs. Finally, the business plan should describe the resources needed to make this happen; the amount of money that the business will generate; and, importantly, over what period of time.

Stage 2: Finance. Having an aspirational business plan is one thing but in practice this will need to have a "reality check" in matching the business's financial aspects to that of the proposed plan. This stage will also determine when money is required and whether it needs to take the form of loan capital or other forms of funding including identification of potential funding sources, for example venture capital.

Stage 3: Implementation. It has to be said that the first two stages do nothing for the business without the task of actual implementation. This stage in the business planning production should provide the organization's management with guidelines for running the business efficiently and introduce the fact that new processes or changes may be needed and how such changes will be programmed and managed.

Stage 4: Monitoring. As a development from any quality process, the business plan, once in place and being used, will need to be monitored to allow the organization's management to assess and control the company's progress by comparison with actual and financial projections in the plan.

From a properly conducted corporate strategic review and business planning exercise involving the board of directors and senior managers, the organization will:

- Gain a thorough understanding of the business, its environment, its strengths and weaknesses, its opportunities and threats and as such have a realistic overview of the business.
- Gain a shared vision of where the company is going, its goals and how they will be achieved. This will provide a sense of direction and purpose.
- Gain an understanding of the key decisions in the business and the part that each department will play

in achieving the required results. As such this will encourage working as a team.

- Have reviewed each key contact with customers, suppliers, investors and so on, and will know what to look for to help support the business.
- Have formed the basis of a system for objective setting enabling each section of the company to contribute to business performance.
- Be better positioned to respond quickly, intelligently and effectively to new situations as they arise.
- Be better placed to secure the financial backing required to implement its plans.

EXAMPLE BUSINESS PLANS

Although there is no set formula for the contents of a business plan, typical examples are provided as a beneficial reference point for those tasked with the production of a business plan. The following five examples illustrate that these may range in detail and how each can vary according to the complexity of the business, its range of products or services, whether it is new or established and the size of its market and competitive position. These example business plans commence with a simple approach to evolving through more detailed plans to the final example which is a very detailed plan structure. However, all of these may be used, in whole or in part, as a template by those producing their organization's business plan. Indeed, for those who do so with an external customer assessor, funding assessor or recipient in mind – bank, shareholders or investors and so on – then adopting a common format is likely to convince the lender that the organization at least knows how to articulate its business and ambitions in a professional and recognizable way.

Business plan example 1:

1. Executive summary
2. Nature of business
3. The product or service
4. The markets and competitors
5. The marketing plan:
   • Market research
   • The target market
   • The competition
   • Marketing methods
6. Operations
7. Financial forecasts
8. Financial analysis
   Appendices, SWOT, PEST, for example.

Business plan example 2:

1. Introduction
2. The business
3. Market information:
   3.1 Products and services
   3.2 Market
   3.3 Competition

3.4 Advertising and promotion activities

3.5 Prices and margins

3.6 Sales plan

4. Location

5. People

6. Capital expenditure

7. Finance:

7.1 Viability

7.2 Direct costs

7.3 Funding

Business plan example 3:

1. Introduction:
    *   Details of the venture – new or established
    *   The nature of the undertaking
    *   The management team
    *   The competition
    *   The size of the marketplace
    *   The extent to which the business is dependent on suppliers
    *   The projections and financial history
    *   The level of investment required and a proposed exit route

2. Background:
    *   The company's background and track record.

3. Products/services provided

4. Management and organization:
    *   The management structure
    *   Staffing plan

- Commitment to company success, financial and otherwise (including share bonus and other arrangements)
- Extent of reliance on outsiders such as lawyers, non-executive directors, and new skills required for company growth

5. Markets and marketing:
- The market: who the major customers are, and why
- How the organization plans to find, and reach, potential customers
- How much bearing the marketing budget will have on the business's success

6. Methods of operation:
- Provision of services: actual/potential problems in provision process
- Present/projected capacity
- Proposed quality/efficiency controls
- Present/future employee need, the availability of relevant skills and current/projected labour costs.
- Premises and facilities: current/future suitability of premises
- Vulnerability to rent or leasehold pitfalls (as opposed to property ownership)
- Adequacy of any necessary training equipment – cost and likely date for replacement

7. Financial information and projections:
- The revenue and capital budgets and cash flow forecasts which should be logical and consistent with the rest of the plan

- The realistic assumptions based on current economic conditions
8. Other information:
   - The sensitivities of the projections and the assumptions made
   - Is there any reason to doubt the soundness of the projections (e.g. historical results)?
   - The details of when the break-even point reached
   - The alternatives and an intended exit route
   - The risks involved in the implementation of the business plan

   Appendices.

Business plan example 4:

1. Introduction:
   - Business plan benefits
   - Outline of business plan
2. The business and its management:
   - Corporate objectives
   - Mission statement
   - Management structure and key individuals
3. Marketing:
   - Marketing plans and product development
   - Market analysis
   - Market share and competition
   - Distribution, sales and promotion
4. Product management:
   - Current products

- Product development
- Product planning
- Infrastructure support

5. Forecasts and financial details:
   - Operating costs
   - Income and profit forecasts
   - Financial risks

6. Phase-related business plan with a programme of future actions

7. Business planning assumptions
   Annex of supporting information covering economic and industrial review of home country.
   Appendix of financial details.

Business plan example 5:

1. Executive summary:
   - Business concept
   - Company market potential
   - Management team
   - Distinct competencies
   - Required funding and its use
   - Exit strategy

2. Company description:
   - Mission statement
   - Summary of activity to date
   - Current stage of development
   - Competencies
   - Product/service description
   - Benefits to customer
   - Objectives

- Keys to success
- Location and facilities
- Differences from current offerings

3. Industry analysis:
   - Entry barriers
   - Supply and distribution
   - Technological factors
   - Economic influences
   - Regulatory issues

4. Market analysis:
   - Overall market
   - Market size and growth market trends
   - Market segments
   - Targeted segments
   - Customer characteristics
   - Customer needs
   - Purchasing decision process
   - Product positioning

5. Competition:
   - Competitor profiles
   - Competitors' products
   - Competitor market share
   - Competitors' services
   - Competitive evaluation of product
   - Competitive advantage
   - Competitive weaknesses
   - Future competitors

6. Marketing and sales:
   - Products offered
   - Pricing

- Distribution
- Promotion
- Advertising and publicity
- Trade shows
- Partnerships
- Discounts and incentives
- Sales force
- Sales forecasts

7. Operations:
   - Product development
   - Development team
   - Development costs
   - Development risks
   - Manufacturing (if applicable)
   - Production processes
   - Production equipment
   - Quality assurance
   - Administration
   - Key suppliers
   - Product/service delivery
   - Human resource plan
   - Facilities
   - Customer service and support

8. Management and organization:
   - Management team
   - Open positions
   - Board of directors
   - Key personnel
   - Organizational chart

9. Capitalization and structure:
   - Legal structure of company
   - Present equity positions
   - Deal structure
   - Exit strategy

10. Development and milestones:
    - Financing commitments
    - Product development milestones
    - Prototype testing
    - Launch
    - Signing of significant contracts
    - Additional funding
    - Expansion details
    - Break-even performance
    - Other major milestones

11. Risks and contingencies:
    - Increased competition
    - Loss of a key employee
    - Regulatory changes
    - Supplier's failure
    - Change in business conditions

12. Financial projections:
    - Average inventory
    - Sales forecasts
    - Balance sheet
    - Income statement
    - Cash flow statement
    - Break-even analysis
    - Key ratio projections

- Financial resources
- Financial strategy
13. Summary and conclusions
    Appendices:
    - Management resumés
    - Competitive analysis
    - Sales projections
    - Any other supporting documents

Having invested time, effort and cost in producing a business plan with its objectives clearly articulated, its distribution should not be limited purely to the senior management or the organization's shareholders, but should be used as part of the day-to-day business and updated as new environmental opportunities and threats arise. This business tool can be used to keep track of current performance and development plans (as shown in Figure 2.4, Stage 4). It should be stressed that business planning should not be thought of as a one-off isolated event but adopted as a lifecycle-based approach; it needs to be used, reviewed and periodically repeated to ensure that the business is achieving it desired level of performance – a link back then to the cyclical, iterative planning process shown earlier in Figure 2.1. The organization will need to measure the business results, costs and success (or failures) and report these against the business plan and its implementation programme. With such knowledge it will be able to modify its products and services as required and make business changes on an informed basis. In addition, it must also monitor the external environment including the competition and any political, economic and social issues, and technological, legal and environmental (PESTLE) developments which may impact on its business operation. In the longer term it will also need to build upon its strengths and the opportunities identified, and address any perceived weaknesses by tactically positioning itself to respond to new threats. A final point to end the benefits of business planning is to consider the quotation of General Dwight D. Eisenhower:

plans are nothing; planning is everything

In the business context this may be taken to mean that the largest benefit is the actual process of planning and the level of thinking that this engenders, rather than just looking at an end product.

BUSINESS PLAN FEASIBILITY

Having listed the above benefits it is a very useful to examine and test the integrity of the organization's business plan following its production – which is likely to be derived as a result of the strategic analysis, marketing and market/product analysis as discussed later in other chapters. It is proposed that success in business depends on three crucial elements; namely, the actual management of the business; its approach to marketing; and the amount of money that the business needs and will generate

Management	Does the management team have the motivation and skills to deliver the products/services you envisage?
	Does the management team have the skills to look after the administration side of the business, including all of the money matters?
	Has the organization the ability to sell the products or services to the potential clients identified?
	Is the management team prepared to modify the business plan in the light of what people want?
	Is the company confident that it is able to manage skills and time to full effect?
	Does it need any new people to make this plan work?
	Does it need "different" people to make the plan work?
	Can the plan work and the business carry on if current key people leave the company for another job, retire, win lottery, etc.?
Marketing	What is so special about the products or services that the company intends to provide?
	How does it know that anyone will want to buy them?
	How often will they buy from your company?
	How much will you charge for the services and are people/companies prepared to pay those prices?
	Are you sure that you can provide these services at these prices, make a profit and manage the cash flow?
	Why should anyone buy from your company rather than another in the market?
	Is this the right time to start providing the product/services that you have in mind?
	Will you be able to develop them further as the market develops?
	Have you considered how you will advertise or promote the company's services and how much will this cost? (See also "'Money" below)
	Where will you advertise or promote the product or services?
	Do you know who the competitors are and what services and products they are selling and at what price?
	Have you spoken to any potential customers about the company's services or goods that you provide now or intend to provide?
Money	Will the business make a profit?
	Will you be able to pay each bill as it arrives?
	What financial resources will you need to be successful?
	Are you confident that you can pay back any loans over a reasonable period, and also pay the accumulated interest?
	Have you researched, listed and costed the expenditure items that you will incur?
	When will income start to flow?
	Which part of the market provides the revenue?
	Is this market secure or high risk?
	What are customers prepared to pay for the company's services/goods?
	What revenue can you expect from new markets?
	What revenue can you get from repeat business?
	What is the cost of acquiring new sales in bidding, making contacts, marketing, presentations, etc.?

Figure 2.5 Business plan feasibility check.

From *The Essential Management Toolbox: Tools, Models and Notes for Managers and Consultants*, S.A. Burtonshaw-Gunn, 2008. Reproduced with permission.

through its operation. Each of these three elements are detailed in a checklist as Figure 2.5 which may be used by the organization to test the feasibility of the proposed business plan and provide the company with a level of confidence before it presents its plan to any external investor or stakeholder. Whatever the size of the organization, its level of maturity, the markets in which it currently operates or plans to operate in, or whether it is a private or public sector organization, this feasibility check with a keen focus on these three key business features is universally applicable.

To end this chapter it is stressed that after the production of the business plan, testing its feasibility using the above checklist, gaining approval by the organization's board or trustees, and investors as appropriate, the business could still fail to deliver its benefits if the business plan is not implemented and consistently reviewed as previously discussed. In addition, a poorly executed business plan at this final stage will destroy the appetite for others to assist in the required future business planning activity if this is not regarded and seen to be valuable to the business operations.

CHAPTER 3

PRODUCT DEVELOPMENT

INTRODUCTION

This chapter looks at product or services development with an obvious linkage to the other chapters of business planning and supply chain management. Product development can take either one of two approaches: it may be a modification to an existing product with a focus on market sustainment, or it may produce market disruption by offering new products or significantly enhanced features such as simplicity, ease to use, lower costs and so on. After some general considerations, both of these approaches to product development are explored in further detail. Whilst the focus is generally on physical products, many of the models and narrative can be equally applied to the provision of services.

UNDERSTANDING PRODUCTION

A good start to understanding product development is first to consider the three traditional "classes of production", these being:

- Primary production which is the earliest stage in the production process such as that witnessed in mining, farming, oil extraction, tree-felling, etc.
- Secondary production involves converting the primary production raw materials into finished, or part-finished, goods either through constructing, manufacturing or other forms of processing.
- Tertiary production describes the activities of the services sector of the economy with examples such as retail, insurance, banking and direct services to the public such as policing, nursing, etc. which rely on the products of the two above classes to create their working environment.

Product management as a necessary part of production can be undertaken as a management activity in any of the above three "classes of production" and is widely regarded as a collective term used to describe a broad sum of diverse activities performed in the interest of delivering a particular product to an intended market. It needs to be undertaken from a business perspective to assist both the long-term survival of the business and in gaining a short-term competitive advantage. A strong example of this is witnessed by car manufacturers' constant attention to product development by modifications and subtle evolution changes ("facelifts") to existing models, and more radical development of future models; even to the extreme of development work on concept-only models to test styling and feasibility ideas. However, it also needs to be stressed that as important as product development is, it does comes at a cost and needs to be aligned with the business plan and market research knowledge. As such the launch of a revised or new product needs to be carefully planned, not just in the lead time that it takes to develop the new item for production but importantly the timing of the launch relative to the sales and market position of current products and competitor dynamics. This is shown on the typical product lifecycle graph, Figure 3.1, where the product sales and market penetration increase over time from its launch to maturity of its market position. Products beyond this point decline to have only moderate sales until their withdrawal.

The Boston Consultancy Group portfolio matrix model shown as Figure 1.6 in Chapter 1 can be used to produce a useful model of product lifecycle combining the above time-base graph with the product market information, as shown in Figure 3.2.

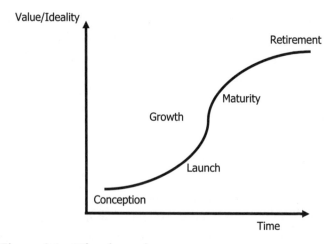

Figure 3.1   Lifecycle graph.

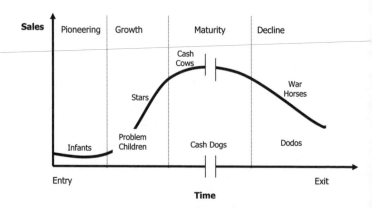

Figure 3.2   Product lifecycle combined matrix.
From "Portfolio analysis and the product life cycle" by H.C. Barksdale and C.E. Harris, published in *Long Range Planning*, pages 74 to 93. Copyright © Elsevier, 1982.

The terms in Figure 3.2 are explained as follows:

- "Infants" are in a position where research and development (R&D) costs are being recovered with high promotional expenditure in terms of educating the market.
- "Problem Children" are in a high-growth situation but with a low market share. They are costly to maintain and market, requiring action to transfer them to "star" or "cash cow" positions.
- "Stars" have high promotional costs but have a good future potential once the product/service has been accepted by the market.
- "Cash Cows" earn money in high market growth/low-growth situations. Another benefit is that promotional costs are lower as the market is already familiar with the product or service.
- "Cash Dogs" are products with a low market share in a saturated market. These typically have uniform cash flow.
- "War Horses" are products in a declining market but which still have a relatively high market share probably as a result of competitors departing the market in favour of new products.
- "Dodos" are products which are in a declining market with a low market share and a negative cash flow. Clearly, these should be deleted from a company's offerings as soon as practicable.

The tasks involved with this topic should cover product planning and the marketing of a product at all stages in its lifecycle. Indeed, from a practical perspective, product management can comprise two professional disciplines: product planning and product marketing, although some companies often perceive them as being one discipline, which they call product management. In general, organizations depend on the abilities of their product management team to:

- perform activities to satisfy customers' requirements utilizing five main areas of product management, namely: people, product, process, plant and programme, with the objectives of balancing a range of needs, such as the need to minimize cost and maximize quality; and
- maximize the use of the plant yet minimize inventory and stock holding levels; and at the same time satisfy the identified requirements to efficiently and effectively meet customer needs (see also Inventory Management in Chapter 4).

These activities are often achieved through a joint marketing/engineering/manufacturing effort depending on the stage of the product lifecycle.

The relationship between marketing and engineering is illustrated in the technical lifecycle shown as Figure 3.3, which aligns the relative effort of both disciplines with the product lifecycle ranging from conception and its "cutting-edge features" through to the product's maturity and eventual decline. Whilst this model shows a uniform separation between the engineering and

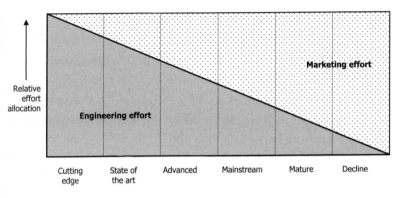

Figure 3.3   The technological lifecycle.
From "Industrial market behaviour and the technology lifecycle"
in *Industrial Management and Data Systems*, Nov./ Dec. 1986.
Reproduced with kind permission of Emerald Publishing.

marketing effort allocation, in practice there will be some
overlap and duplication depending on the product, the
company's working philosophy and the individuals
involved. To expand on Figure 3.3 further, the product
lifecycle phases are described below:

- Cutting edge: Technology product marketed without
  specific application.
  No target market.
  Sales in technology markets.
- State of the art: Adopt cutting edge to meet wider
  market needs.
  Sales based on technological benefits.
  Begin to sell on benefits.

- Advanced: Product's concept adopted.
  Sales based on benefits.
- Mainstream: Low-cost, high-quality standard product.
  Sell on benefits.
  Segmented market.
- Mature: Reduced product differentiation (commodity market).
  Shift from segmentation to customer service.
- Decline: Displaced by new technologies.
  Price competition.

As companies look for improved performance, one method of supporting this is to identify and eliminate waste, look to lean production principles developed by Japanese industry (primarily in the car giant Toyota), and examine products from a number of interpretations of the term "value" discussed below.

CONSIDERATIONS ON "VALUE FOR MONEY"

Apart from the occasional rash, hasty, impulsive decisions as private individuals, we choose to make purchases of goods, services or even various leisure pursuits based on a variety of criteria. Typically, these range from affordability in relation to our own budget, to functionality from our judgements on quality and our expectations of reliability. In addition to these practical considerations is the influence of the aesthetic appeal and in some instances there is also the perceived status of ownership. These buyers may be classified as:

- Innovators – first to buy, risk takers.
- Adoptors – purchase when product is a success and entering next stage of product lifecycle.
- Sceptics – late majority who buy when product idea is well tested.
- Traditionalist – only buy when product is fully established and moving to decline phase of lifecycle.

The consideration of aesthetic appeal and ownership status can contribute to an equation of investment versus benefit, and hence support the concept of the term "Value for Money" (VfM). In respect to the supply of goods in particular, consideration may also have to be made with respect to the longer-term running/upkeep and maintenance costs ("cost of ownership") and the product's residual value ("cost of disposal") which will also include an amount of depreciation or even appreciation in some rare circumstances. In looking at how companies, government or public institutions operate, it is only right and fair to expect a similar assessment for their purchase of goods and services especially if funded through the public purse in the case of the latter. Within the UK government, spending can be subject to a review by the independent National Audit Office who stress the importance of value for money by using assessment models such as the Public Sector Comparator (PSC) or Private Sector Shared Services Delivery model.

It is suggested that the concept of VfM is not as straightforward as may first appear as the notion of "value" may offer a range of subjective alternatives against investment considerations. In this case it is necessary to make a clear separation between the monetary cost of an item and its value and to this end the prudent financial advice of the 19th century art critic, poet and social commentator, John Ruskin, remains as valid today as when first published over 100 years ago:

> It's unwise to pay too much, but it's unwise to pay too little. When you pay too much you lose a little money. That is all. When you pay too little you sometimes lose everything, because the thing you bought was incapable of doing the thing you bought it to do. The common law of business balance prohibits paying a little and getting a lot. It cannot be done. If you deal with the lowest bidder, it is well to add something for the risk you run. And if you do that, you will have enough to pay for something better.
>
> **John Ruskin (1819–1900)**

Following on from this advice on cost and value and therefore with a proposal that the term "value" can be expanded from a pure financial measurement into other areas, these are now discussed and explored further in general terms in Figure 3.4.

Value . . .	Example of good practice	Example of poor practice
The value of the customer–supplier relationship	Supplier understanding of customer's wider requirements, culture and how the product will be used with a desire to jointly be associated with a successful project and longer-term relationships.	Constantly changing people, unable to develop any rapport, trust or interest in wider user's issues. Little or no interest in repeat business.
The value of product development	Ability to specify features required (e.g. new computers, factory fitted car accessories).	Unable to change specification as goods are already made to meet mass market appeal ("take it or leave it approach")
The value of subsequent design change flexibility	Main agent/dealer recall on motor car safety developments. Dealer-fit accessories.	Products are unable to accept new modifications (e.g. computers) and have to be completely replaced.
The value of product/services reliability	Goods need little maintenance, always performs as required.	Goods break down or become faulty during or soon after warranty period expires.
The value of product/services availability	Choice of goods, models, features available in showroom, ready to take away.	Goods need to be ordered as demand exceeds supply so there is a long waiting list (e.g. key toys at Christmas). Although for some niche products such as specialist cars, for example, low availability provides a level of exclusivity and perceived value.
The value of product/services performance	Goods and services perform as required in line with marketing literature (e.g. car fuel consumption figures).	Goods and services do not perform as required. Products wear out soon after warranty period expires.
The value of lifetime product/services support	Established dealer network with spare parts, service centres and after-sales care support.	Goods soon become obsolete and after a relatively short period of time are no longer able to be maintained or serviced, for example computer hardware products.
The value of safe product operations	Goods meeting UK and EU safety kite standards, e.g. cycle helmets.	Second-hand electrical goods of unknown origin (e.g. when bought from car-boot sale).
The value of product use training	Knowledgeable sales staff, good after-sales service, online help desk, product instructions, etc.	Poor instructions for use, no product training or awareness by sales staff.

Figure 3.4 Proposed product/services "values" with examples of good and bad practice.

Value . . .	Example of good practice	Example of poor practice
The value of product maintenance	Easy to maintain, no special tools required. Maintenance thought through at design stage.	Design not undertaken with longer-term maintenance in mind making this difficult or a need for special tools. Building design may need specialist scaffolding to allow routine maintenance activities.
The value of the product or services adherence to programme requirement	Online internet shopping with delivery of goods to home.	Delivery dates delayed due to problems with production, raw materials, etc.
The value of residual worth	Desirable quality items retain a high residual value (e.g. specialist watches, "exotic" sports cars).	Low worth after use. Many consumables are in this category.
The value of a status feature	High price, limited number of unique or bespoke products (designer clothes, haute couture).	Increased market demand allows price reductions to allow mass-market appeal. (Top brand clothes sold in supermarkets.)

Figure 3.4   Continued.

Figure 3.4 provides a wide range of examples of the term "value" and it has to be appreciated that the value of the product or service is conditional upon circumstance; this value often reduces when the need has been satisfied or the service or product is considered surplus to an immediate, perhaps urgent, requirement. However, the opposite is also true: when the need for the product or service is absolutely paramount the concept of "value" may then defy any reasonable financial assessment criteria. The flexibility of this conditional supply and demand concept is best seen in Shakespeare's famous line taken from the play "King Richard III":

A horse! A horse! My Kingdom for a horse!
William Shakespeare King Richard III,
Act 5, Scene IV

Even this royal plea for a simple commodity at a grossly exaggerated cost assumes that in "value" terms the horse will be able to perform, be reliable, be safe, be of the correct "specification" for its required task and is immediately available without further delay. Notwithstanding that decisions on a like-for-like basis are often made by financial comparison (and where the advice of John Ruskin shown earlier is most applicable), a wider range of the term "value" presented in Figure 3.4 is now used as a foundation to assess "value" in respect to an example product, in this case a new defence platform (aircraft) programme. This is shown in Figure 3.5 to prompt similar considerations that can be applied across a wider product range. Using this may also identify a competitive advantage which could feature as part of an organization's marketing or customer management strategy.

Having explored the possibility of assessing the value of goods against a range of criteria other than an initial cost or purchase price comparison has provided an alternative assessment for VfM considerations. With an acceptance of this approach it would be possible to assign a score against each of the "value" categories and thus establish a total score and a lower "fail" limit. A practical example of this could be on scoring the value of "reli-

For the example defence product	Demonstration of meeting this value	The consequences of not meeting the value
The value of the customer–supplier relationship	Partnered approach fundamentally covering **hard** (development of solution and deliverables) and **soft** (team working, behaviour, joint decision making, performance monitoring) **issues**. A partnering charter could be used to support best industrial collaborative working practice and further demonstrate a commitment to joint working.	Traditional arm's-length contracting will act to strengthen an adversarial approach of claims and counterclaims for cost and time delays for both information requirements and hardware delivery. A poor supplier–buyer relationship will develop which will impact on time, cost and quality and also the morale of the supplier's staff on the project in working with the procuring customer.
The value of product development	Joint buyer and supplier design and development team engaged in product development. Close involvement with supply chain members.	Aircraft, equipment and systems could be developed in isolation of the customer by the manufacturers and in ignorance of the end user's needs or how the products will be used. Such working is not likely to result in products that conform to the customer's operational requirements.
The value of subsequent design change ability	Ability to consider future needs and plans for upgrades as part of a modification management service.	Aircraft and systems will in time become obsolete or even the equipment fitted may not meet with the customer's changing defence requirement without additional modifications. This may mean that its future operational ability will be lost or reduced if future defence developments cannot be incorporated with its operational capability.
The value of product/services reliability	Testing and reliability modelling of product. Identification of improvements.	If either the aircraft structure or the performance of its equipment is not reliable then its operational status cannot be guaranteed on which the government may base land, sea and air defence decisions.
The value of product/services availability	Performance management established to examine and plan aircraft availability and training systems availability.	If the aircraft, its systems or its equipment are not available to meet the operations requirements, this lack of defence capability is likely to impact on the effectiveness of national security.
The value of product/services performance	Fleet management and business/performance management/availability performance management. Development of aircraft testing carried out with full customer participation and shared addressing of results.	If either the aircraft product or its systems and equipment do not perform to the required specification this will impact on the effectiveness of the defence capability and national security.

Figure 3.5 Example product/services "values" considerations for a new defence (aircraft) project.

For the example defence product	Demonstration of meeting this value	The consequences of not meeting the value
The value of lifetime product/services support	Programme includes the provision of pre-planned product development to achieve flexibility in equipment capability over its design life.	In terms of defence capability the aircraft and its associated systems and equipment will not be capable of performing its long-term intended role as its technology becomes outdated, obsolete and fails to provide the necessary operational requirements.
The value of safe product operations	Safety is managed by an integrated customer and supplier joint organization. Strict adherence to the applicable airworthiness and safety regulations and responsibilities of both parties is planned and maintained through the delegation of authority to appropriate members of the joint buyer–supplier team.	Unlike the other "values" safety of operations is not just a requirement but mandated in state legislation. Indeed, this requirement will extend to flight crew, service support personnel, i.e. maintenance and ground service engineers and all civilian population under the aircraft's flight path. Whilst 100% safety cannot be guaranteed any risks will need to be managed. Unsafe practices and operations will lead to injury.
The value of product use training	Recognition that the aircraft programme caters for the provision of specialist training equipment and programmes to meet customer in-service preparation requirements.	Without the necessary training the customer will be unable to use the aircraft, systems and associated equipment to its design potential and in a safe and effective manner.
The value of product maintenance	Aircraft programme includes maintenance management services with a provision of long-term support from joint industry/customer organizations as applicable.	Without the necessary aircraft and systems maintenance the customer will be unable to use the aircraft, systems and associated equipment in a safe and effective manner. In addition, it will be unable to have any confidence that the aircraft and equipment will be able to perform as and when required.
The value of timing	Buyer and supplier working together to develop a smooth transition with respect to the operational and in-service capability as the new aircraft is delivered to the customer.	Whilst this "value" is related to achieving the delivery of the aircraft and associated operational equipment, training and ancillary support to the buyer's programme, the consequences of a delay in achieving the stated in-service dates imposes additional costs to the customer in maintaining any current capability from other aircraft. Thus delay in the new aircraft programme will result in an additional burden on current operations.

Figure 3.5 Continued.

For the example defence product	Demonstration of meeting this value	The consequences of not meeting the value
The value of residual worth	Joint understanding that this element is unlikely to be a feature in any "'value" consideration as the end of life disposal of the aircraft is unlikely to generate an income. However, this is not to dismiss the sale of the product (aircraft) before its economic end of life operations. In this case the asset will have a residual worth although the market for it may be limited and as such the financial value difficult to establish at an early stage.	Aircraft has limited value to anyone beyond current customer, apart from its scrap material worth or approved third party revenue opportunity.
The value of a status feature	Although the element for the aircraft is not a true feature within this "value" consideration, it may represent a major improvement on the customer's current capability and is regarded as a state of the art product.	Aircraft has a poor reputation as a low status capability and is not taken seriously by customer, and in other armed forces, this is likely to reflect on the state standing on the international stage.

Figure 3.5 Continued.

ability" when − irrespective of any other value − product reliability is deemed to be imperative to the performance of the product. In other words, and using a different product example, what is the value of a perfectly balanced, technically advanced, superb road-holding rally car with a world-class driver if it consistently fails to start or routinely breaks down?

Adopting a quantitative approach to VfM does not necessarily mean that all of the criteria need to achieve the maximum score, but could be used to identify where the customer's product or services specification can be met by current market availability or highlight where future product or services development needs to target identified customer expectations. This understanding of the customer's need and joint product or services development strengthens the VfM values of "product development" and "subsequent design change ability" shown in the above tables. It also contributes to providing increased supplier performance which is likely to result in higher levels of customer satisfaction.

EXISTING PRODUCT DEVELOPMENT

It is said that some of the major problems in modern living are too much noise, too much information, too many decisions, too much complexity, together with issues on quality and reliability. Addressing these problems in connection with existing products may provide welcome improvements to them and is often a far more cost-effective option than the more expensive new product development. Examples of development opportunities with respect to existing products are shown in Figure 3.6 and are partly suggested by the Russian problem-solving technique "TRIZ".

In many cases existing product development will be a continual process of evolution such as seen in car design, with prototypes and through to production models. Few innovations come from their development by inventors in their spare bedrooms, garage or workshops; in reality most successful innovations are born, bred and brought to market within well-established organizations and with the benefit of significant financial resources.

Product development suggestions	Example products
Simplification by removing complexity	Ready prepared fresh-food meals
Apply the existing product to a new use	Combined scanner/photocopier/fax machine
Automate	Electric kettle, toaster
Reduce cost	Mass-produced items, TVs, Compact Discs, computers
Make easier to use and understand	Cameras and picture processing
Reduce fear to own, use	Chain saw, hedge trimmer
Give more performance such as capacity	Jumbo size flask
Make faster, less waiting for customer	Instant coffee, lottery tickets online, internet banking
Provide more durability and improved reliability	Motor cars
Design to give better appearance	Stay-pressed fabric, water-proof clothing
Add new features and functions	Multi drink machines – coffee, tea, cappuccino
Make portable	Sony Walkman, then to MP3 players, iPods, etc.
Make easy to clean or self-cleaning	Self-cleaning ovens, self-de-icing freezers
Make operationally quieter	Vacuum cleaner
Integrate functions	Mobile telephone with digital camera and MP3 player. Blackberry, iPhone
Make more flexible and versatile	Vacuum cleaner attachments, suitcases with wheels, mobile phones with cameras
Make lighter weight – or heavier if this implies better quality	Hover lawn mower, garden furniture
Make smaller	Mobile phones, collapsible umbrellas
Make larger, if this improves user interaction	Plasma screen television
Make more powerful	Computer processors
Reduce or eliminate drawbacks or side-effects	Medicines, no-drowsy tablets
Make more accurate	Quartz watches
Give better shape, design, style	Kitchen goods
Provide better sensory appeal (taste, feel, look, smell, sound)	Digital radio
Provide better psychological appeal (understandable, acceptable)	Branded "fashionable" goods
Provide better emotional appeal (happy, satisfying, enjoyable, fun, etc.)	Sports equipment such as skateboards, surf boards, roller blades, etc.

Figure 3.6 Existing product development options.

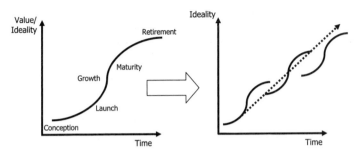

Figure 3.7 Product lifecycle "S" curves.

The life of a single product was shown earlier in Figure 3.1 where the value to the organization is plotted against time; this is a typical product life profile. Existing product development often follows the right-hand graph of Figure 3.7, where the company has a series of developments which are introduced after maximizing the return of each subsequent version; this is very typical of motor car manufacturers where the same product name remains constant. These are sometimes marketed as Mark II, III, VI or Series II, III and so on depending on the manufacturers' preference up to a runout model. Clearly, there is a point on the graph where the car manufacturer has both the existing and the new models available and whilst often they discount the existing version to clear the old stock they also keen to have a visible presence of the new model in the market. Often the additional features are small when compared between the two versions and typically the main differences are aesthetic design changes, themselves deliberately planned to "date" the current version. Over the last 20 years, Japanese electronics, particularly hi-fi but also computer games, have followed the same graphs although at a much faster rate than that of a typical motor car example.

Some companies benefit from a systematic approach to continuous improvement in both their operational processes and product updating; this may be set out in a continuous improvement plan. Product development in the context of Figure 3.7 is often a combination of some new elements and enhancement to the existing product portfolio. As such the following "rules" may be useful for those tasked with considering product continuous improvement:

1. Continuous means ongoing and as such the process itself should never stop although will have resource and budget implications.
2. Once a year, it is advisable to have an outsider review the business approach as they can often see what you cannot. From a practical viewpoint some formal confidentiality agreement will need to be established, for example the use of focus groups.
3. It is often suggested to do the simple and cheap things first and quickly. Concentrating on what is referred to as the "low hanging fruit" builds credibility, momentum and commitment within the organization. It may also provide the opportunity to

practice where such learning may be useful in the future.

4. Do not try to do it all at once. It is advisable to set up a plan and undertake the implementation in stages.

5. Try to work on two or three top priorities as working on more can diffuse effort, energy and resources.

6. Celebrate, acknowledge and reward accomplishment. This itself creates a positive environment for improvement.

7. Make certain that improvements involve the organization's customers with a focus on delivering increasing value.

8. Look for breakthrough improvements. A number of small incremental improvements can result in a major overall improvement.

9. Develop a continuous improvement system that works for the specific business. Do not copy others without considering first your organizational setting, culture and business model. Often what works for one business will not work for another.

10. Look inside your industry and at the competition to seek out examples of best practice. Competitors can often show you a better way and if it works after testing then adopt, adapt and improve it to suit your business.

The above list of continuous improvement was drawn up for larger organizational development rather than for a range of products; however, it is clear that the lessons from this are equally applicable to existing product development.

NEW PRODUCT DEVELOPMENT

Introducing a new product to the market is seldom easy; it is often time and resource consuming, especially as it will need some level of legal protection to prevent direct copying by competitors and the route through the patents application process will often require specialist help. Trade-offs made to deliver one level of value cannot deliver another, therefore the organization's value chain is different and its competitor's business model is often not easy to replicate. From research it is said that for every 5000 raw ideas 500 are actually progressed and 50 feasibility studies are undertaken. Indeed, from these the organization may be fortunate to find five products to launch and in the main only one of these will be successful. As such, in the words of 3M's Art Fry, inventor of the Post-It note:

> You have to kiss a lot of frogs to find a prince.
> But remember, one prince pays for a lot of frogs.
> **Source: "Innovation in industry",**
> **_The Economist_, November 1999**

When it comes to formulating a new product development strategy, there are four potential avenues of innovation:

- Existing market growth – making improvements to existing products and services.
- Related market growth – improving existing products and services to provide added features.
- New market creation – creating a new product or service for customers to meet an identified need.
- Disruption – covering the creation of a product or technology that enables a new set of customers to use the product to perform a job that only specialists could previously do.

Although market growth in all areas is always an important feature of new product development, most companies concentrate on their existing market and are often reluctant to pursue the other avenues of growth even though they may offer higher returns. Success in the creation of a new market can offer significantly more profit than success in the same market; however, this also always attracts a higher degree of risk. As such, to achieve a well-balanced new product development strategy, a company's resources should be allocated as follows:

- 60% on existing market growth.
- 20% on related market growth.
- 15% on new market creation.
- 5% on disruption products.

Having mentioned the term "risk" above, Figure 3.8 illustrates the relationship of product and market from a risk perspective. In marketing terms new business or sales

	Same product	Extended product range	Incremental change	Totally new product
Existing market	Low	Low	Medium	Medium
Related market	Medium	Medium	Medium	High
Totally new market	Medium	Medium	High	High
Market disruption	–	–	–	High

Figure 3.8 New product, market and risk.

can come from existing or new customers; for existing customers the approach is one of "farming" by investment of time and building strong relationships. Alternatively, attracting sales from new customers is more akin to "hunting" as the effort is considerably more onerous to achieve the required result. This rationale is widely seen in the abundance of customer loyalty schemes in use to retain customers and hence secure their repeat business. The risk of "hunting" has clear parallels with the risk of products and markets shown in the figure. This is not to suggest that the high risk strategy should be avoided; only that a mix of the two approaches is likely to provide the best overall results (see also Figure 4.7 in Chapter 4).

New product development demands the management and coordination of three main functions, as shown in Figure 3.9. The inter-relationship of these three functions stresses that a weakness in any one of these areas is likely to result in overall failure of the new product, for example if the design is flawed or not properly resolved it will be difficult for marketing to promote it. The design needs

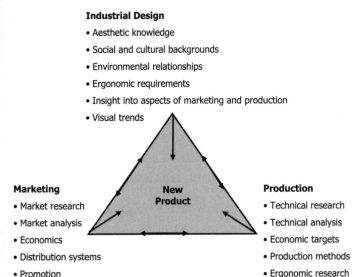

Industrial Design
- Aesthetic knowledge
- Social and cultural backgrounds
- Environmental relationships
- Ergonomic requirements
- Insight into aspects of marketing and production
- Visual trends

New Product

Marketing
- Market research
- Market analysis
- Economics
- Distribution systems
- Promotion

Production
- Technical research
- Technical analysis
- Economic targets
- Production methods
- Ergonomic research

Figure 3.9 Management of design.
From *The Essential Management Toolbox: Tools, Models and Notes for Managers and Consultants*, S.A. Burtonshaw-Gunn, 2008. Reproduced with permission.

to reflect production capabilities and even if the design itself is superb and the production world class, without professional marketing its sales will be limited at best and more likely nonexistent. The elements of the product from a marketing perspective typically consist of not just function, variety, quality, design appearance, its features and branding, but also customer after-service, warranties and product guarantees. Indeed, the "Management of Design" model suggests that it is these three disciplines which are linked together through the development of a new product, these being production, marketing and industrial design, where each function has a valid contribution to bring to the design process to see this through to customer sales in the chosen target market.

The design of a product employing the three key elements of Figure 3.9 needs to consider differentiation, in other words identifying the features which will distinguish this product from others; there are a number of ways that this may be achieved such as:

- Features – capabilities of the product or service.
- Fit – tailoring the product or service to suit customer requirements.
- Styling – functional, visual, tactile.
- Reliability – warranties, lifetime guarantee, returns policy of product.
- Packaging – colour, size, shape, protection.
- Sizes – clothing, appliances, computers and luggage sizes.
- Brand naming – labelling, implied status or meaning.
- "Turnkey" solutions – total ownership solution, funding, service, warranty, disposal as seen in the growth of personal car lease arrangements.

Throughout this chapter it should be clear that the subject of product development has a clear relationship with the large and important topic of marketing; further tools and approaches will be presented in detail in the future book *The Essential Tools for Marketing*. However, in ending this chapter one way of analysing the oppor-

Market type	Market demands/export opportunities
Developed world	Higher technology
	Unique features
	Sophisticated distribution
	Superior promotional support
	Well-developed back-up and support
	For consumer products, a clear difference (objective and subjective) when compared with local suppliers
Underdeveloped world	Medium and lower technology especially capital plant
	Good support, especially technical
	Limited luxury goods
	Specialist consultancy services
	Basic distribution (through physical distribution can be a problem)
	Limited promotional support
	Longer-term finance
	Local manufacturing opportunities
Developing world	Technology for licence agreements/local manufacture/investment
	Finance
	Luxury goods
	Medium- and high-technology imports
	Good distribution
	Good promotional and technical back-up

Figure 3.10 Export markets.
From *The Handbook of Management*, page 324, 3rd edition. Gower Publishing, 1992. Reproduced by kind permission of the editor Dennis Lock. Copyright © Dennis Lock.

tunities that exist in different export markets with respect to product development is to divide the target countries into three broad zones as shown in Dennis Lock's table reproduced as Figure 3.10, where each zone offers opportunities for a wide range of products or services. Careful analysis needs to be made of the options open to a company for entering into each country/zone balanced against the organization's own strengths and weaknesses. Such consideration should then allow the organization to make informed decisions about the attractiveness of any particular export market. Typically, to penetrate an export market the products must have strengths in at least one of the following:

- Technical specification.
- Reliability.
- Simplicity.
- Specialist application.
- Aesthetic features.
- Price.

In conclusion, the topic of product development can be seen to comprise product design balanced with an understanding of customer needs and importantly getting the design product or services in front of the target customer to make the sale, generate a profit and use this to invest in further product development to replace aging products or launch new development concepts. These should be in line with the organization's business objectives and gaining the support of suppliers and staff will be crucial to the success of this management function, and hence the natural importance of the following chapter topics. Finally, although the major emphasis of this chapter has been on physical development, as suggested in the introduction much of this chapter is also relevant to those involved in the provision of services.

CHAPTER 4

SUPPLY CHAIN MANAGEMENT

INTRODUCTION

Organizations have to recognize, respond to and satisfy the requirements of their customers if they intend to stay in business and benefit from future growth through repeat business. In support of this, supply chain management (SCM) has, for many companies, developed from the older function of purchasing to now embrace planning, implementing and controlling all of the suppliers to the organization with a view to delivering a more integrated service to its customers. This is often achieved

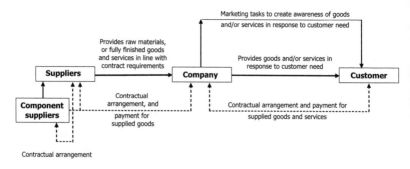

Figure 4.1   Elements of the supply chain process.

though both vertical and horizontal integration. Typically, the management of the supply chain includes raw material ordering, storage, work-in-process inventory and finished goods. Such management is achieved through a set of product and production processes covering commercial, financial and quality management activities. Through this integrated approach, SCM offers organizations a systematic approach to the management of its entire value-added chain; from the component level supplier to the main manufacturer, integrator or prime contractor, then to the retailer who in turn finally exchanges the goods for money with the end customer (Figure 4.1).

This chapter examines the development of SCM and the relationship between the supply chain members together with some approaches to customer relationship management which is naturally linked to product development discussed in the previous chapter. At one time the key phrase was "customer satisfaction", then there followed a period where companies aimed to "delight" their customers and more recently there has been a broader move to managing customer's expectations known as "customer experience" in services and products which suggests closer contact with the customer base through proactive communications aimed to gain a closer understanding of their present and future customer requirements. Whilst SCM is growing in popularity, this management function is not without some challenges. The rationale for this chapter is to provide information to as wide a readership as possible and as such the specific SCM elements of detailed logistic and returns management are outside of this scope.

THE DEVELOPMENT OF SUPPLY CHAIN MANAGEMENT

The relative power of the supplier in relation to the buyer's business and vice versa need to be considered in the light of SCM as the performance of each party will have a direct impact on the other's business. Traditionally, the purchasing function of the organization has focused on "playing the market" to achieve short-term cost savings; however, over the last decade many companies have recognized the hidden costs of retaining a plethora of small suppliers with all of the associated administration that such numbers necessitate. Whilst there be a natural reluctance to be reliant on a sole supplier arrangement, as a compromise, organizations have moved to

selecting a small number of suppliers with which to
develop fewer, closer relationships as part of a fundamen-
tal shift towards long-term working. The transition from
a simple purchasing function into SCM has also witnessed
a cultural change where much closer cooperation is seen
between the supplier and the buyer; this is very evident
in the UK's retail, manufacturing and to a lesser extent
construction sectors. The latter has previously been
renowned for its adversarial relationship; however, over
the last 15 years this too has seen dramatic changes resulting in a more collaboration through "partnering" where
both parties commence their business relationship by
agreeing a set of mutual objectives, have an agreed process
for problem resolution and decision making, together
with a joint commitment to continuous improvement
and performance measurement.

One definition of SCM and its development is:

> A way of thinking that is devoted to discovering tools
> and techniques that provide for increased operational
> effectiveness and efficiency throughout the delivery chan-
> nels that must be created internally and externally to
> support and supply existing corporate and service offerings
> to customers.
>
> **From Cox, A. *Supply Chain Management*, 1999**

In looking closer at this type of relationship, partnering can be applied to one-off schemes (commonly referred
to as "Project Partnering"), or can be ongoing over a
series of developments (often called "Strategic Partnering")

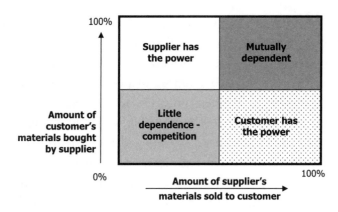

Figure 4.2 Buyer–supplier relationship.
From *The Essential Management Toolbox: Tools, Models and Notes for Managers and Consultants*, S.A. Burtonshaw-Gunn, 2008. Reproduced with permission.

intended to govern a long-term relationship based on an agreed trading formula. Within SCM terms an obvious partnering relationship is worthy of consideration when a mutual dependency between a supplier and a customer exists, as shown in Figure 4.2; conversely, where there is little or no dependence between suppliers and customers due to market size or the number of suppliers, there is rarely an advantage in committing resources to develop this type of closer working relationship. At the extreme relationship level it must be said that care has to be taken to ensure that through partnering arrangements a legally binding agreement between the participants is not created which would require additional legal considerations of both a statutory and regulatory type.

With well-established supply chains many parties in the arrangement have a level of security of future work and hence a confidence to commit investment to staff development through training; in plant and equipment; and, finally, to business processes to support the SCM relationship. Other developments in SCM typically centre on reducing inventory, increasing the transaction speed by exchanging data in real time, and increasing sales by implementing customer requirements more efficiently. With increasing globalization of business operations and use of worldwide suppliers, SCM will continue to increase in importance. As such it is a particularly important feature that needs to be considered by those companies seeking growth through international operations and/or expansion into new international markets.

SUPPLIER–BUYER RELATIONSHIPS

Depending on the business sector there will be a range of issues which determine the importance of the supplier to the buyer. In some businesses, the goods or services provided by a supplier may be substituted with different models, etc.; be replaced by those of a competitor; or discontinued on instruction of the buyer. The model shown in Figure 4.3 examines this from a buyer's perspective where the relative position of the customer–supplier dependence is based on the value that each has on one another's business performance. Understanding

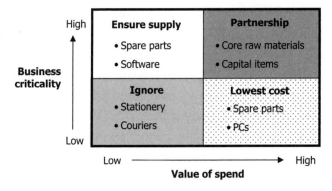

Figure 4.3 Trading between supplier and customer affecting importance of relationship development.
From *The Essential Management Toolbox: Tools, Models and Notes for Managers and Consultants*, S.A. Burtonshaw-Gunn, 2008. Reproduced with permission.

this information can be useful for companies to recognize the strength or vulnerability of their supplier relationships and to assist them in setting business or operational strategies. As an example such relationships are also seen in the much publicized Japanese "Keirutu" financial and industrial groups in which cross-ownership networks contractually tie buyers and suppliers together over long periods. Indeed, SCM itself has seen a significant growth over the last decade resulting in recognition of its strategic importance and the competitive advantage that this branch of management can offer.

An alternative, less formal, approach is for organizations to develop capabilities to be able to meet the requirements of current and future customers and instead of forming a joint venture, benefits may come from closer working within their respective supplier base. This supply chain approach usually prompts a series of cost and quality improvements which can in turn lead to the creation of more satisfied customers and hence increase the opportunities for repeat business.

The pressure to pursue partnering as a key source of collaborative advantage has to be traced back to the different historical stages of the concept of "outsourcing" as we know it today. As the market for outsourced services has matured so the requirement to seek more innovative operational philosophies has given credence to adopting partnering as a key corporate strategy in increasing profitability and additional shareholder value. This move towards collaborative working has meant a significant change for some organizations to their business operations, as seen in Figure 4.4; whilst for others such change has been more easily accepted and undertaken.

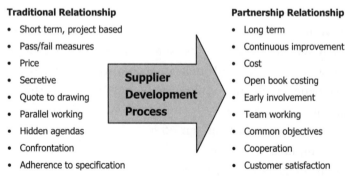

Traditional Relationship
- Short term, project based
- Pass/fail measures
- Price
- Secretive
- Quote to drawing
- Parallel working
- Hidden agendas
- Confrontation
- Adherence to specification

Supplier Development Process

Partnership Relationship
- Long term
- Continuous improvement
- Cost
- Open book costing
- Early involvement
- Team working
- Common objectives
- Cooperation
- Customer satisfaction

Figure 4.4 Strategic transformation through collaboration.

Therefore to fully understand the performance benefits of partnering it is useful to recognize the historical market developments in outsourcing. Within what are termed the "first generation" arrangements between customers and suppliers in the early 1990s, the relationships which existed then allowed typical profit margins in excess of 20% to be gained as a result of using outsourced resources. Many of these focused heavily on the removal of a problem for a customer and were grounded in the provision of safe and fairly low-risk quality solutions. However, new entrants through either start-up or diversifying organizations began to flood into what appeared to be a lucrative market, with low barriers to entry and attractive and accessible profit levels. At this point the need to collaborate as an essential element of business performance was only partially appreciated. The growth in the outsourcing market was by now so rapid that by the mid-1990s the intense competition in this provision gave rise to "second generation" arrangements which centred on cost-driven solutions; in the case of the UK government contract arrangements this promoted a move away from traditional "cost-plus" contracts towards those on a fixed-price basis and sometimes on more elaborate "availability-based" and incentivized contractual arrangements.

In all collaborative working arrangements there will be a number of key items that both parties will have to discuss and agree to take the relationship forward, these typically will cover the following list which will be useful to those new to establishing a partnering relationship, and equally be a good reminder for those who have done this before as a best practice checklist:

1. The production of a **Statement of Principle** where it is documented that Companies A and B agree in principle to work together in an open and trusting style in partnership deliberately to create a business relationship which is ethical and progressive, delivering tangible, measurable benefits to both partners over a long period.
2. Agreement of the **Scope of the Partnership** to which the relationship extends, this could be sharing of materials, services, intellectual resources and knowledge.
3. Detailing of the **Service Standards** – for example, that the supplier will work to ensure achievement of customer performance and service levels of not less than x% timeliness of delivery, y% quantity of delivery and z% quality of delivery.
4. **Technology** – each partner will work to improve the technology and process of manufacture of the materials and items supplied and will regularly review specifications to ensure maximum effectiveness of items supplied.
5. Both parties will establish a **Continuous Improvement Programme** in their own businesses, apply it to the items supplied and meet regularly to assess potential improvements.

6. Each partner will set and agree specific annual **Objectives and Oligations** of task performance and will further agree to review these together.

7. Where **Capital Investment** is required to be undertaken this will need to be identified at the beginning of the relationship and the criteria for investment, payback and return on the investment will be clearly agreed before any investment is made.

8. A **Confidentiality Agreemen**t will need to be drawn up to cover the exchange of any contentious or sensitive technologies or information between the two partners. This agreement should also be an absolute obligation that such information is not disclosed to any third party of any kind.

9. Sometimes that is also an **Exclusivity Agreement** where investment is made in proprietary tooling or specialist technology developed between the two parties where supply to a third party may not occur without the specific written agreement between the partners.

10. Production of a **Termination Arrangement** which needs to be agreed at the outset in the event that all other avenues are exhausted and both partners wish the relationship to be dissolved.

11. Agreement of **Management, Communications and Publicity** – which is used by each party to brief its management and staff regularly on the nature of the agreement and the status of the relationship between the two parties.

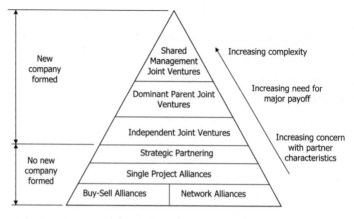

Figure 4.5 The range of collaborative working options.
From *Essential Tools for Organizational Performance*, S.A. Burtonshaw-Gunn and M.G. Salameh. John Wiley and Sons, 2009.

12. **Key Contacts** will be listed who have responsibility of managing critical key relationships between the partners and specific companies.

Having already mentioned a number of partnering types, the range of collaborative options is shown in Figure 4.5 and discussed in more detail in *Essential Tools for Organizational Performance*.

Whether in the short or long term, central to any successful collaborative supply chain relationship is the willing involvement of all parties and the belief that together they will realize significant benefits above and beyond what is normally achievable within the boundaries of a standard provider–supplier contractual commitment. This development is often a natural step arising from an established existing relationship between companies that have previous successful experience of cooperation together. However, for such benefits to be possible requires openness, honesty and above all a desire for continuous vigilance by all parties to identify further areas for development and growth within the value chain of the business arrangement. In these relationships the concept of trust is a key element to its success and is often developed in the parties passing through the following four stages:

1. Where the mindset is not to trust anyone.
2. Where the mindset is not to trust anyone until they prove themselves.
3. Trust people but only until they make a mistake.
4. Trust people even after they have made a mistake.

Accepting that this negative approach is often a general starting point some suggested actions aimed to build a trusting relationship are:

*   To go first and lead by example.
*   To illustrate the topic by drawing on relevant examples, without "telling".
*   To listen for what's different and not what's familiar.
*   To be sure your advice is being sought before offering your views.
*   To earn the right to offer advice.
*   To say what you mean.

- To ask for help when you need it.
- To show an interest in the person and what is important to them.
- To respect other cultures if different from your own.
- To use compliments not flatter.
- To show appreciation.

Establishing good, close and strong supply chain relationships – not just formal partnering – is the ideal way for any company to conduct business; however, this is not without risk and the risks of supply chain management and such collaborative working are shown in Figure 4.6.

This model covers the main features of environmental risks, client and supplier risks, project attractiveness and the competitive risks taken from Professor Michael Porter's widely used model of competitive analysis discussed earlier in Chapter 1. Understanding these risks can be used to develop the relationship within the supply chain, whether at the client, lead consultants or specialist contractor positions, where each party can gain an appreciation of the risks that the other supply chain partners face and have to deal with.

Systematic risk management begins with recognizing the risks in order that their potential can be quantified and mitigation activities taken to eliminate or at least reduce their impact. Within some partnership arrangements, notably in the UK construction industry, there has been a focus of establishing three key features of the

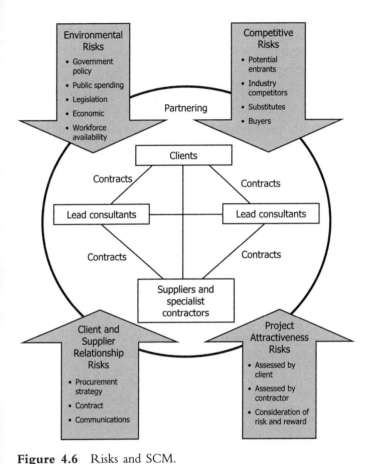

Figure 4.6 Risks and SCM.
S.A. Burtonshaw-Gunn, page 107 in *Supply Chain Risk*. Editor: Professor Clare Brindley, 2004. Reproduced with permission of Ashgate Publishing.

arrangement, namely: identification of the mutual benefits; a problem resolution process to be used prior to any contractual claims; and a commitment to continual improvement. Embracing these three key features will clearly contribute to relationship building from the outset, assist in the promotion of a long-term relationship based on trust and hence minimize cost and time over-runs through better, less formal and more proactive communications.

Whilst partnering as a concept may then be regarded as a success, the contribution of risk management in this relationship clearly plays a significant role. Indeed, it is suggested that the consequences of failing to manage risk has an impact not only on the organizations involved, but also on individuals and may result in:

- Significant project over-runs.
- Schedule delays.
- Inability to achieve stated technical objectives in terms of delivery, functionality, costs and so on.
- Project de-scoping.
- Project cancellation.
- Penalties and fines.
- Personal and/or organizational liability.
- Loss of credibility for company and for individuals involved.

It has to be recognized that some collaborative alliances fail; in the main this is down to just two causes. Either they are flawed from the outset:

- By being poorly conceived, given a changing competitive situation.
- Through a lack of complementary objectives.
- From being the wrong type of alliance.
- Through a lack of commitment to the relationship by staff or senior management.

Or they go wrong over a period of time:

- As parent companies drift apart due to changing priorities.
- By poor management of the alliance at the parent company level.
- By poor management at the alliance level.
- Through a lack of commitment to the relationship by staff or senior management.

In order to minimize failure, six suggestions are proposed:

- Learn about each other before you start.
- Get beyond national or local stereotypes.
- Explore, do not ignore, the differences.
- Create a spirit of equality.
- Identify and focus on shared objectives.
- Recognize limits to culture change.

The model shown as Figure 4.7 is developed from studies on both risk and trust where the characteristics of each quadrant are detailed. This is a useful tool for people to understand and identify the relative positions of all

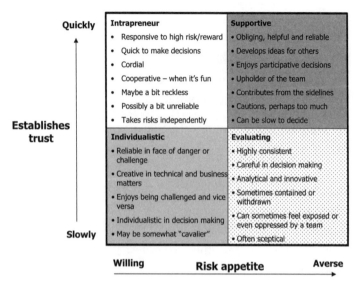

Figure 4.7 Risk and trust in SCM.

members of the partnership or supply chain; how they behave now; and how they may need to change in the future.

Having so far discussed the stages and some of the key points which need to be considered in forming a closer working relationship within an organization's supply chain members, on occasions this may have a finite life such that at the end of the joint undertaking – project, product launch, service provision, etc. – it will be necessary to draw the arrangement to a close. Whether this is a planned and agreed decision, or as a result of a breakdown of the partnering undertaking, the stages shown in Figure 4.8 will be applicable to both. This is

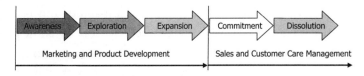

Figure 4.8 Partnership lifecycle.
From *The Essential Management Toolbox: Tools, Models and Notes for Managers and Consultants*, S.A. Burtonshaw-Gunn, 2008. Reproduced with permission.

included to demonstrate that even after a successful relationship such an ending may be natural and indeed beneficial for both parties allowing them to learn from such experience for the benefit of future business opportunities.

When the partnership relationship is in progress there are three key elements: commitment; mutual advantage and opportunity; and trust, which all need to be present. Indeed, without these the partnering relationship is unlikely to be successful. These key elements are detailed below:

1. Commitment: Those companies partnering must commit to a long-term relationship as this results in a stable relationship which is not in a state of constant reassessment and in which each partner has a clear focus on continuous improvement and dedication to common goals. The commitment to partnering should come from the highest levels of authority in each organization; there are two good reasons for this. First, the decision to partner is of great importance, especially to the client who may lose some of their technical capability and has to place a great deal of trust and reliance on its chosen partner. To make these changes and decisions, commitment is required at the very highest levels within both supplier and customer organizations. The second reason is related to when the two organizations are working in partnership. If the perceived benefits of the collaboration are not happening as quickly as anticipated, the attitudes of the staff and management may change towards partnering and the arrangement may start to falter.

This is where the commitment to partnering from the top management is essential, as it is the senior management who need to maintain the momentum of the partnering process by encouraging and motivating their staff until the benefits can be seen. When the commitment to partnering is made it should be strongly and widely communicated to all the stakeholders and their employees and the whole project community. Commitment to partnering must come from top management and be visible, supportive and ongoing; it must be a genuine commitment – not just lip service. Apart from commitment, each organization should appoint at least one individual who will be totally dedicated to the concept of partnering and who, through dedication and enthusiasm, will ensure the successful implementation of partnering within the organization and beyond. This "partnering champion" maintains the focus on the goals of the project and the partnering process, and will guide people through a maze of the day-to-day issues.

2. Mutual advantage and opportunity: The partnering companies should expect more advantages and more opportunities than are available in traditional business relationships commensurate with their investments and risks. Project goals are generally set by the client during the concept development stage of a project's life, to reflect the partnership's end user's needs. An examination of current practice shows that members of the project team have little or no input into the development of these goals, but are required by contract to adopt them as mutual project goals. Alternatively, the client's goals have often been poorly communicated to project participants, largely due to inadequate brief development. This practice has meant that where problems arise on the project, because there is little commitment to or understanding of the necessary project outcomes, satisfying the project goals has become secondary to safeguarding individual organization's interests. In a partnering process, each stakeholder's interests are considered by creating a set of goals that satisfies their requirements for a successful project. At a partnering workshop, for example, the stakeholders identify all respective goals for the project in which their interests overlap. These jointly developed and mutually agreed-to goals may include:

- achieving value management savings;
- meeting the financial goals of each party;
- limiting cost growth;
- limiting review periods for contract submittals;

- early completion;
- no lost time through injuries due to safer working practices;
- minimizing the amount of paperwork generated;
- no litigation; or
- other goals specific to the nature of the project.

3. Trust: A partnering relationship is unable to succeed without a strong element of trust. Throughout the development of personal relationships and communication about each stakeholder's risks and goals a better understanding is developed and with such understanding engenders the value of trust. Indeed, establishing trust serves to combine the resources and knowledge of the partners in a fashion intended to eliminate adversarial relationships. Within partnering, trust is therefore important for two particular reasons. First, since a partnership is intended to continue over a long period, each party makes a considerable commitment to one another; as such the reliability and integrity of their partner is paramount. Second, a successful partnering relationship requires each organization to share its strategies and possibly proprietary or confidential information. Each company must therefore respect the other company's needs for confidentiality of any shared information.

The success of partnering fundamentally relies on stakeholders conducting business in an open and trusting way. Creating these relationships begins with respect for others, from which trust and in turn a collaborative team approach emerges. On the other hand, teamwork is not possible where there is cynicism about others' motives. Through the development of personal relationships and communications about each party's risks and goals, there will be better understanding.

INVENTORY MANAGEMENT

The final part of this chapter covers inventory management. With production of "goods" there will be a need for the purchase of raw materials, raw material stock control, managing work in progress (WIP) and the management of finished goods stock, prior to point of sale. Irrespective of the company and product range there will always be the need to balance holding too little or too much stock in the form of either raw material or finished goods. Whilst the organization's finance people often want to have the least amount of money tied up in stock, the balance is not just a company decision, as the market also has a role to play. Bespoke goods for customers, car specifications, made-to-measure suits, etc., can only be in raw material form until customers order them; on the other hand, cars can be made ready for sale, as can ready-to-wear suits, and although both may still attract buyers, they do so on a "take it or leave it" basis.

In looking at the reasons for holding stock, any one of five main justifications can be made, these are termed:

- Pipeline – where inventory is on hand to minimize production delays and maximize efficiency.
- Cycle – suppliers have minimum order amounts that are greater than immediate need.
- Safety – stocks held to avoid a shortage because of uncertain production demands. Stockout (i.e. having zero stock) is expensive if it causes production to be halted.
- Anticipatory – where inventory is held in anticipation of known demand.
- Speculative – items purchased to beat supplier price increases.

The most effective stock ordering system must be aligned to the organization's marketing strategy; however, in many cases the usage of raw materials being transformed into finished goods follows the model shown as Figure 4.9.

In efficient companies, materials arrive in time for production – for example, the "Just in Time" (JIT) technique famously originated in Japan where the cost of holding stock was reduced to the minimum; however, there are risks with this approach concerning the security of their delivery. JIT can be achieved through a combination of long-term contracts, frequent deliveries, short response times, improved communication through transmission and zero defects. The car manufacturer Toyota has described its own JIT system as achieving the items it needs for production at the necessary time and in the

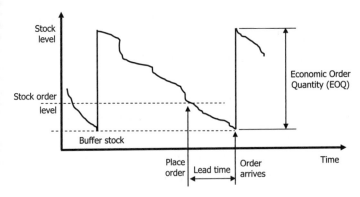

Figure 4.9 Stock ordering strategy.
From *The Essential Management Toolbox: Tools, Models and Notes for Managers and Consultants*, S.A. Burtonshaw-Gunn, 2008. Reproduced with permission.

right quantity. It supports lean manufacturing by seeking to eliminate "muri" (overburden), "mura" (unevenness) and "muda" (waste) in their manufacturing processes. For some companies who are unable to have guaranteed supplier deliveries, the alternative is to hold large amounts of stock in case there is a delay in new raw materials arriving so that this will not affect production; this was a common approach some 20 years ago and since then the trend has been a compromise by holding and ordering the most economic quantities. This supply chain approach comes at a cost, including the cost of processing this stock held in stores or as work progresses, and the money invested as well as cost of operating the stores. Other supply chain costs are:

- The cost of processing goods or the purchase price of goods.
- Set-up or changeover costs.
- The cost of materials handling.
- The cost of transport and internal transit.
- The cost of packaging and promotion.
- Administration and communication costs.
- The costs of failure or reduced sales caused by stockouts and failure to deliver on time.
- The cost of tariff duties where international movements are concerned.

The cost of holding stock is obviously a function of its amount, how difficult it is to store and its longevity. This is shown in Figure 4.10.

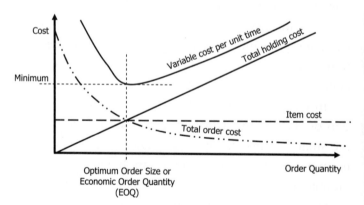

Figure 4.10 Variation of cost with order size.
Model taken from *The Handbook of Management*, page 428, 3rd edition. Gower Publishing, 1992. Reproduced by kind permission of the editor Dennis Lock. Copyright © Dennis Lock.

The EOQ formula tries to find that optimal point at which the total cost of both ordering and carrying is minimized using the formula:

$$EOQ = \sqrt{\frac{2 \times R \times O}{C}}$$

R = Annual units required
O = Cost of placing an order
C = Cost of holding a unit of stock per period

The formula calculates the most economic inventory order and hence the number of orders per year. The advantage of reduced stock holding is naturally a corresponding reduction in storage facilities, complete with their associated costs for lighting, heating, security, insurance and so on. However, the EOQ formula is only of real benefit when the demand is constant, when demand fluctuates wildly perhaps due to seasonal variation or fashion demands then this is of reduced value. Sophisticated computer programs exist that perform a modified calculation more frequently to adjust the EOQ for fluctuating demand projections.

In ending this chapter it is hoped that the contribution of SCM to operations management is recognized, as the strategic importance of this topic is gaining further prominence in the role of business planning and organizational and competitive performance. Whilst at the operational level, SCM continues to cover stock and inventory control, at the higher level the increase in supply chain partnering is now widely recognized as a business enabler although one that has implications for individual and team behaviours as discussed in the final following chapter. As such, this important area of management has a clear role to play in all topics of operations management covered in the previous chapters of business planning, strategic management and product development, especially where this requires a closer working relationship with suppliers and end-users.

CHAPTER 5

PEOPLE MANAGEMENT

INTRODUCTION

This final chapter recognizes that key to the operation
and success of businesses is the role of people in undertaking both individual and team activities. As such, whilst
the wider topic of human resources management (HRM)
typically covers recruitment, selection, development,
policy setting, etc., it is noted that for some larger companies this may be outsourced to a professional HRM
service provider leaving in-house retained HR staff in a
more advisory governance role with little capability or

authority to interpret operational policy to suit business unit or individual circumstances. In this way outsourced HR delivers operational strategy with the retained HR staff ensuring compliance with corporate governance. This chapter focuses not on these policy undertakings but on behavioural management aspects of people from both an individual and team performance basis. It also presents a view on task management which is a key operations management activity drawing on both individual and team actions and suggests that the attributes of project management may be seen as an example of task management in action.

The leadership task is to effectively undertake three inter-related activities; in John Adair's Action-Centred Leadership model this is represented by three circles representing the core management responsibilities of achieving the task, building and managing the team or group and, finally, managing the work and development of individuals. Whilst the team leader will have to assign tasks, build the team and play a role in the development of staff, it should also be noted that high-performing teams also exhibit the same regard for task, teamworking and self-development opportunities.

The structure of this chapter reflects John Adair's model by covering the three overlapping areas of individual, team and task management (Figure 5.1). In addition, it ends with some guidance on dealing with team conflict.

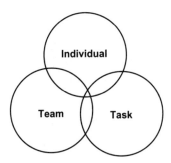

Figure 5.1 Action centred leadership: balancing task, team and the individual.
Model reproduced by permission of John Adair from *Effective Leadership*. Published by Pan, 1988.

MANAGING INDIVIDUALS

Managing the needs and expectations of staff is not just providing more economic rewards such as salary, bonuses, etc. but is a balance between other inter-related activities of job satisfaction and the social relationship with other members of the organization (Figure 5.2). However, in looking at economic rewards, performance-related pay is widely regarded as an important element in many performance management schemes because it strengthens the message that performance and competence are important and provides a mechanism to reward people according to their individual contribution and competence. That said, there is also a corresponding view that such economic rewards can actually inhibit teamwork because of their individualistic nature, and as such can lead to the

Figure 5.2 Needs and expectations of people at work.
From *The Essential Management Toolbox: Tools, Models and Notes for Managers and Consultants*, S.A. Burtonshaw-Gunn, 2008. Reproduced with permission.

de-motivation of some team members through their perceptions of the performance and disparate reward of other team members.

In managing individuals it is often their specific needs and expectations that in many cases can only be partly fulfilled by economic rewards, thereby requiring a greater focus on job satisfaction, respect and appreciation for contributing to an organization's future performance and their own developmental challenges. As such setting and agreeing action plans and development opportunities for individuals will be an important management task for those responsible both for individual staff and team performance.

There are a number of HRM tools which can be deployed to contribute to enhancing performance often necessitating joint actions of managers and their staff, with a view to improving individual and hence organizational performance. The process of objective setting is almost uniformly used either on an annual basis or on a task basis as appropriate. Setting realistic and achievable objectives can be used to improve performance, although for maximum benefit the Plan-Do-Check-Act process should also be used to support periodic review and monitoring. As an example the following individual development approaches are used in many companies.

- **Performance development reviews (PDRs):** Whilst PDRs may be used in the management of an organization's performance, even those companies without performance management systems tend to operate staff appraisals in which managers are required to review staff performance, their potential and identify their development needs. Those organizations with PDRs also use this time to reflect on the individual's past performance as a basis for making development and improvement plans. Review meetings should be constructive and conducted in an open, free-flowing and honest way and where the reviewee is encouraged to do most of the talking. At the same time as reviewing competent performance, a number of organizations also choose to conduct an assessment of the individual's behavioural competencies as part of their performance management system. Such a behavioural assessment can provide another consistency tool for measuring individual performance and for providing development activities to help employees further reinforce their technical skills and interpersonal competencies to reflect the organization's required practice standards. Although the process allows time to access individual performance it is not appropriate to use this to surprise staff with unfounded criticism or impose unrealistic objectives when they may be at their most vulnerable.

- **360–degree feedback:** This review mechanism consists of performance data generated from a number of sources and almost always includes those staff to which the individual reports, their peer group, their staff and, in appropriate circumstances, their customers. This approach typically includes a self-assessment using a common process to allow the individual's own perceptions of their performance to be compared with the other assessing groups. The 360-degree feedback approach is widely used as part of a self-development or management development programme, where a more rounded view of the individual is required and with less bias than if such an assessment is conducted only by the individual's immediate line manager.

- **Objectives and performance standards:** Here both the manager and the individual will need to agree on a number of objectives or goals that can be undertaken by the individual, department and organization over a period of time, usually in a one-year period so that they may be aligned with the appraisal or performance review timescales. These objectives can be both work-related, referring to the results to be attained, or personal objectives, taking the form of developmental objectives for individuals. In both cases, however, objectives must be regarded as "SMARTT" (Specific, Measurable, Agreed, Realistic, Time Bound and Traceable) and may be expressed as targets to be met or tasks to be completed. Setting SMARTT objectives, reviewing performance and providing feedback to individuals are key stages of a typical performance management system. From either the PDR review or indeed any other process of setting objectives it will be important to recognize that this is likely to be a mixture of mandatory and discretionary objectives, as shown in Figure 5.3.

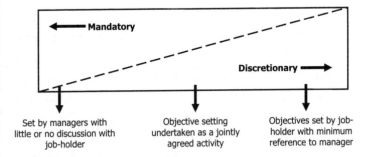

Figure 5.3   Achievement objective.
Model taken from *The Handbook of Management*, page 904, 3rd edition. Gower Publishing, 1992. Reproduced by kind permission of the editor Dennis Lock. Copyright © Dennis Lock.

- **Teamworking:** For many organizations teamworking has become an important part of contributing to its business success. In instances where projects justifiably allow for team membership to be long term, then team performance (output, customer service, customer satisfaction and financial results) can be measured. However, these will require team members to agree on their objectives and receive feedback on their individual contribution to the team and/or project.

- **Coaching:** For some managers, the provision of coaching is an important tool in assisting to develop an individual's skill set and knowledge. For the individual it can result in improved job performance and the achievement of wider organizational objectives. Coaching can often be part of the individual's learning and development and may be addressed in their PDR. Unlike the performance review process "Coaching" usually takes place throughout the year and often features executive development ranging from the directive, company mandated requirements on executives, through to a number of more empathetic approaches such as coaching, supporting and counselling on an "as and when required" basis.

- **Learning and development:** In almost every business the main route to improved organizational performance is the improvement of individual skills and competencies. This will require an understanding of the processes and techniques of organizational, team and individual learning and the PDR is often the ideal time to encourage individuals to think about which ways they wish to develop. This should result in establishing a personal development plan with agreed actions, budgets and support requirements against which staff can develop themselves in line with the company's business objectives. Away from company initiated development, learning and development can also include self-managed learning, which is widely regarded as a process whereby individuals determine what they learn and how they do so in the context of their own situation.

- **Senior management development:** It is important to consider the context within which learning and development resides within an organization, especially as there will exist a continuum of aspirations ranging from economic survival, through to maintenance and business growth, with success at any of these stages dependent on the right organizational development decisions being made. Of course, whilst this argument can be applied to all levels of an organization, it is often the senior management who most critically need to have the necessary abilities to contribute to setting and being accountable for achievement of the organization's corporate goals and performance. To appreciate how these decisions can be effectively focused it is important to understand how learning and development needs can be prioritized for the senior management population within a company. Typically, their development falls into the three groupings of maintenance, strategic and career needs, with each being described below:

- **Maintenance needs** are those needs that the organization must address in order to stay in business, for example employment legislation, heath, safety and environment regulations, corporate taxation liabilities etc. Generally, maintenance needs are considered as the "must-do's" of any business and usually comprise a top-up of knowledge and skills to support a steady-state operational environment.

- **Strategic needs** cover the type of needs that should be addressed in order to achieve the corporate goals, some of which will more than likely be centred on business improvement or change management. Examples of strategic needs may include increasing service provision standards and the introduction of new technology, products or services. In contrast to the maintenance needs, strategic needs can be regarded as organizational "should-do's" generally because they tend to relate to business transformation activities relying on the development of new knowledge, skills and even attitudes in order to manage business transition and transformation activities effectively.

- **Career needs** relate to an organizational mindset regarding investing and developing people so that over time they can make a more effective contribution to the company's current and future strategic plans. In this category examples include the need to continuously develop and maintain a level of domain-specific experienced managers with the right competency profiles. In prioritizing learning and development it is often the career needs which are typically thought of as optional and consequently the "could-do's". These tend to realize a return on investment to an organization over the mid to long term and, in many instances, may be driven as much by the individual's own aspirations as any direct organizational requirements. However, this is not to suggest that career needs are unimportant; on the contrary they are often a critical element in supporting the organization's ability to stay competitive and achieve growth.

Having established these three groupings and understood them from a demand and planning perspective, it is then essential to establish where the right balance lies for a particular organization. Whilst consideration may be given to the three categories of learning needs it should be noted that there are also other wider influencing factors which often come into play in assessing the strategic role of learning and development, as shown in Figure 5.4.

Whilst it is important for managers to understand and play their part in the development of their staff, it is also

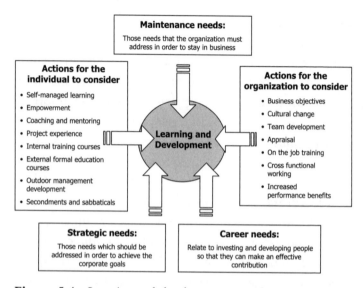

Figure 5.4   Learning and development considerations.
From *The Role of Strategic Executive Development*, S.A. Burtonshaw-Gunn and M.G. Salameh. ICAFI University Press, 2007.

incumbent on them to assign work based on their personal competencies, i.e. skills, technical knowledge and attitude, as this provides a degree of confidence to both the individual and to the company that operations are being managed in accordance with corporate governance requirements. It is suggested therefore that for development purposes, managers may wish to provide new opportunities for their team. However, where on-the-job learning is used to develop staff this will need to be adequately supervised and supportive training provided especially in governed industries. This approach is important to demonstrate to the individual that the training is being provided as part of their planned development, rather than as just as an additional resource undertaking a piece of work.

The final factor in managing staff is in establishing an optimal working relationship which needs to be based on mutual respect, trust and support for one another.

MANAGING TEAMS

A useful starting point in managing people is to consider the definition that a team is a group of people who share common objectives and who need to work together to achieve them.

Whilst performance can come from the empowerment of teams or individuals by managers, it is often a management or team leader function to build teams that are concerned with improving performance and results by making greater use of both individual and team strengths – not simply concentrating on weaknesses. There have been a number of studies on team dynamics and the roles that team members undertake; the most widely known of these coming from Dr Meredith Belbin's 2004 publication *Management Teams* and his subsequent studies. The intent of this chapter is not to detail team working from an individual member's perspective, but to concentrate on how teams may be managed. On this premise the roles described by Belbin provide a useful understanding of how individuals working in a team function and their natural membership characteristics. A brief description of the original team characters and the later study additions are provided in Figure 5.5.

Whilst individual teams may have a degree of empowerment from their immediate manager it is clear that full empowerment, covering rewards, goal setting, appraisals and so on, has to be driven from the top of the organization to become part of the company's corporate culture and business philosophy. Although many organizations may wish to empower their employees, this can present problems – not for those empowered, but more often for their managers who consider this as a "loss of control" and erosion of authority whilst recognizing the benefits of empowerment.

Teams and teamworking may be part of the normal way to operate in a business; however, they consistently offer the opportunity to accomplish much more than the sum of the individual members in getting a job done, extreme examples being sports teams or an orchestral concert. Nevertheless, where the work is more varied, teams may be especially established for a task only and will then break up at its completion, with team members leaving to be part of new teams. A good example of this regular team building and dissolution is on project work where the team share a common goal for the duration of the project and, once complete, then disband. The lifecycle of such team dynamics is shown in the six stages; the first four initially published in Tuckman and Jensen

Role classification	Characteristics
Plant	This role describes a person who is creative, imaginative and an unorthodox team member who excels in solving difficult problems. Whilst often reserved and quiet they are always keen to contribute. It has to be said that their approach can also create a degree of frustration in other team members.
Resource investigator	This role describes a person who is the networker for the group. Whatever the team needs, this person is likely to know someone who can either provide it or know someone else who can help. Such items may be physical, financial or human resources, political support, information or ideas. They are highly driven to make connections with people, and use this ability to support the team.
Chairman	This role describes a person who ensures that all members of the team are able to contribute to discussions and decisions of the team. Their concern is for fairness and equity among team members. Those who want to make decisions quickly, or unilaterally, may feel frustrated by their insistence on consulting with all members, but this can often improve the quality of decisions made by the team.
Shaper	This role describes a dynamic team member who enjoys a challenge and thrives on pressure. This member possesses the drive and courage required to overcome obstacles.
Monitor–evaluator	This role describes a person who is serious, strategic and discerning and who tries to see all options before considering a response. This member contributes a measured and dispassionate analysis and, through objectivity, stops the team committing itself to a misguided task.
Team worker	This role describes a person who is concerned that interpersonal relationships within the team are maintained. They are sensitive to atmospheres and may be the first to approach another team member who feels slighted, excluded or otherwise attacked but who has not expressed their discomfort. Their concern with people factors can frustrate those who are keen to move quickly, but their skills can ensure long-term cohesion within the team.
Completer–finisher	This role describes a "detail" person within the team possessing a great eye for spotting flaws and gaps and for knowing exactly where the team is in relation to its schedule. Team members who have less preference for detail work may be frustrated by their analytical and meticulous approach, but the work of the completer–finisher ensures the quality and timeliness of the output of the team.
Later additions to the characteristics	
Implementer	This role describes a person who is the practical thinker and who can create systems and processes that will produce what the team wants. Taking a problem and working out how it can be practically addressed is their strength. Being strongly rooted in the real world, they may frustrate other team members by their perceived lack of enthusiasm for inspiring visions and radical thinking, but their ability to turn those radical ideas into workable solutions is important.
Specialist	This role describes a person who brings specialist knowledge to the team.

Figure 5.5   Team role characteristics.

in 1977 and the latter two identified through further work. Each stage shows the typical behaviour of its members.

Stage 1: Teamworking is underdeveloped as reflected in the term "forming"; here the group is characterized by anxiety and the main concern for its members is who fits where, who is joining the group and the relative position of each member. Stage 1 signs may include team members being self-conscious, overly polite, embarrassed and enthusiastic but with stilted conversation and little progress made to date. It also has a period of consensus and a dependence on the team leader.

Stage 2: The team is now experimenting and is concerned with how they will work together; this "storming" stage is a natural event even in high-performing teams and even if the members have worked together before. Often roles are challenged and members test one another. If sequentially missed out it will often lead to team problems later which will then need to be addressed before better performance can be gained. Stage 2 signs may be witnessed by conflict, lively debate and discussion, rebellion against the leader, polarization of opinion, members trying out ways of working and tasks beginning to be achieved.

Stage 3: The team is now beginning to work well together having resolved any issues, and areas of conflict are patched up. There is widespread help in the group between its members and the focus now moves to the task and how individuals can help one another. This stage is termed "norming" as norms and patterns of work are established. Stage 3 signs may include shared leadership tasks, a preparedness to change, active participation by all members, mutual problem solving and an open exchange of ideas.

Stage 4: Teamworking is now mature and the fully productive group is said to be "performing" after the other stages have passed. Their main concern is in achieving goals and where help amongst team members is second nature as each knows the strengths and weakness of each other. Roles within the group are functional and flexible. Clearly, this is the position which team leaders aim to get their team to as soon as practicable. Indications that the team is at this stage may be witnessed by a relaxed, purposeful atmosphere, feelings of confidence, goals being achieved and most talk being about the job.

Stage 5: This fifth stage is not in the original work but has been identified later as something to avoid as it relates to "dorming" or falling asleep. It highlights the need to continually involve people in decision making about what they do and how they do it. In practice this stage is likely to occur near the end of the life of the team when people are unsure what they will be doing next; it may be seen as members trying to extend the life of the group.

Stage 6: This final stage on teamwork is termed "mourning" and occurs where the team performance is disrupted by the end of the teamwork, by members leaving to take on new work, by members being uncertain of the future role and generally by the overall break-up of the team, the shared experience and the ending of working friendships. For the team leader this stage is still important as any gradual break-up of the team will reduce the performance overall. Signs of this may include working on tidying up loose ends, celebrating achievement, feelings of sadness and planning for new teams. This final stage is often given less attention than the earlier team-building stages as the main task or project is now completed and as such the central focus of the team is reduced.

For those managing a team, understanding how it is performing and where it is in relation to these six stages are key points to be able to manage its performance and enable individuals to fulfil their required role. In practice managers undertake team building for several reasons such as:

- A team approach is a strong and decisive management style.
- Stress is reduced as problems are shared.
- More ideas are generated, so the capacity to innovate is increased.

- Large or multi-disciplinary problems are better resolved from a team approach.
- Interpersonal difficulties, confusion over roles and poor personal contribution issues can often be resolved successfully in a team.

It is not easy to immediately create a team, as effective teams have to be constructed methodically and the relationships have to be built and developed, work methods need to be clarified and a positive teamworking environment created. The simple checklist below can be used to determine the "operational health" of a team in asking does the team:

- Know where it's going? – this week, month, year?
- Communicate this direction?
- Feel in control of its destiny?
- Communicate on a two-way basis?
- Have opportunities to suggest alternatives?
- Use emotions well?
- Praise people for good work?
- Avoid negative use of emotions?
- Work in a constant mood of fear and depression?
- Have a clear set of standards?
- Accept its standards as being not too high or too low?
- Have an effective hierarchy and an effective distribution of work?
- Freely discuss individual strengths and weaknesses without fear of recrimination?
- Know each other; better than superficially?

- Plan successfully?
- Make the best use of resources – people, equipment and budget?
- Have an identity?
- Complain and moan too much?
- Have a method for resolving disagreements?
- Put emphasis on results?
- Enjoy itself and work together?

For longer-term and strategically important projects, a more detailed look at the teamwork and how this is supported by the organization may be necessary. This can use the COPS model shown as Figure 5.6 with its detailed questions listed below. The benefit of this framework is to provide an understanding of the team's "health" and may be used by managers and consultants

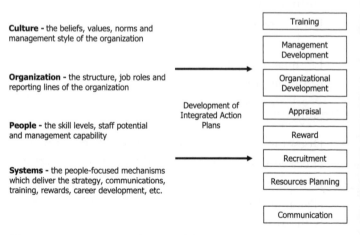

Figure 5.6 COPS analysis model.

to conduct such an audit in a confident and informed manner and be used to identify areas for improvement, change and reinforcement of current practices.

Culture

- Do staff identify with the organization and the success of the organization as being of direct benefit to themselves?
- Do staff see themselves as having common interests with their work colleagues and group?
- Is there a strong team spirit?
- Is work allocated on the basis of individual expertise rather than position in the organization?
- Are your staff encouraged to say what they think about the organization?
- Does the organization encourage innovation and creativity amongst staff?
- Do staff feel a sense of personal responsibility for their work?
- Is quality emphasized in all aspects of the organization?

Organization

- Does the structure of your organization encourage effective performance?
- Is the organization structure flexible in the face of changing demands?
- Is the structure too complex?
- If so in what areas?

- Do staff have clear roles and responsibilities?
- Does the organization structure tend to push problems up rather than resolve them at the point where they occur?
- Do procedures and management practices facilitate the accomplishment of tasks?
- Do you constantly seek to challenge your organization structure?

People

- Do staff have the necessary skills and knowledge to perform their jobs in the most effective manner?
- Do staff understand their jobs and how they contribute to overall business performance?
- Do staff have a customer service orientation?
- Are people with potential spotted and developed for the future?
- Are the staff encouraged to perform well through the giving of recognition, feedback, etc.?
- Do people know what their expected performance standards are?

Systems

- Do your organization's systems (recruitment, promotion, planning, management, information and control) encourage effective performance among your staff?
- Are these systems consistent across the organization?
- Are there clear rewards for effective performance within your work group?

- Does the organization review its systems frequently and ensure they mutually support each other?

In managing teams, the team leader, the team tasks, the experience of the team members, the working environment, and the corporate culture all dictate to a large extent the team leadership style and provide an earlier indicator of future achievable performance. In general this will be a balance between authority and a degree of freedom. This is shown in the popular model of Figure 5.7.

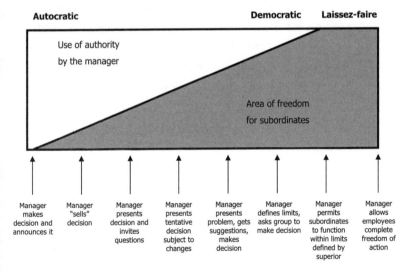

Figure 5.7   Continuum of leadership styles.

Whilst this model shows the full range of the use of authority in decision making, it is unusual to find many examples purely at either end of the continuum although these do exist: autocratic styles deployed in the operational armed forces environment; or a laissez-faire style more aligned to creative therapy. For those teams operating within the "middle ground" the amount of authority/freedom regularly changes with respect to situations, individuals and team dynamics.

In ending this section it has to be stressed that team managers should have a personal commitment to relate to others directly and honestly, as those who use their position for manipulation, demoralizing others or restricting potential, are soon detected and mistrusted. Team members invariably watch their leader's management style and evaluate their ability to promote openness, cooperation and team debate. Without effort, personal integrity and trust, a team cannot be developed to its full potential.

MANAGING TASKS

Although the main focus of this chapter is on people management, as seen in John Adair's model (Figure 5.1), the team leader or manager has not just to manage individuals and the team, but is also responsible for the success of the task. Clearly, this will vary depending on the work setting but in many cases will be a mixture of

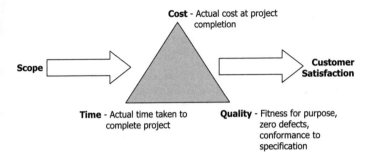

Figure 5.8 A project management approach to undertaking tasks.
From *The Essential Management Toolbox: Tools, Models and Notes for Managers and Consultants*, S.A. Burtonshaw-Gunn, 2008. Reproduced with permission.

working and allocating work, setting budgets and ensuring that tasks are completed within the required timescales and that the work is produced to the right quality. In addition to this it should strive to achieve customer satisfaction whether customers are truly external or internal, often found in large organizations. These main factors are shown in Figure 5.8 which is widely used in the management of projects in various industries.

For those managers undertaking the three elements of Figure 5.1 when considering task management it is suggested that the skill sets shown in Figure 5.9 are needed to help them to identify their own development needs.

Having mentioned the role of the team leader in managing the three action-centred leadership elements,

Management area	Required skills
Operations	Monitor, maintain and improve service and product delivery.
	Initiate and implement change and improvement in service, products and systems.
	Manage finance.
	Monitor and control resources.
Projects	Meet time, cost, quality and customer requirements.
	Manage project risk.
	Safeguard company (and own) reputation.
	Manage safety of personnel.
People	Recruit and select personnel.
	Develop teams, individuals and self to enhance performance.
	Plan, allocate and evaluate work carried out by teams.
	Create, maintain and enhance effective working relationships.
Information	Seek, evaluate and organize information for action.
	Exchange information to solve problems and make decisions.

Figure 5.9   General management skills.

this chapter ends with some text covering the common problem of dealing with conflict within a team setting.

MANAGING TEAM CONFLICT

Although team working can offer major advantages over individual work tasks because of its diversity of resources, knowledge and ideas it may also be the source of conflict. Disputes can arise for different reasons and although every team is unique there are some common patterns to deal with conflict, with the main issues arising from factors such as:

- Poor communications such as a reluctance to share information flow, differences in interpretation and so on.
- Structural factors such as goals and priority issues, the size of the team, levels of participation, reward systems and levels of interdependence.
- Personal factors such as an individual's self-esteem, their personal goals, values and needs.

It is suggested that most managers are aware of team disagreements and may have received training in conflict resolution. However, they are often reluctant to give this a high priority and as such it is often team members that take the lead to resolve conflict among themselves. It should be noted that conflict in teams may not necessarily be destructive as it can be a catalyst for new ideas and approaches to the adoption of new organizational processes and development. However, this will not become so if it is left to escalate to the point where people begin to feel defeated and a climate of distrust develops, which can quickly destroy even an established and well operating team. Potential areas from which conflict issues commonly arise include:

- The team failing to understand or use their administrative processes rendering the team members unable to coordinate their work.
- The team consisting of insufficient resources to undertake the work. Whilst for short spells this may be acceptable, over a longer period there

will be some resentment of being taken for granted. As such it is important that team leaders ensure adequate resources for the work to be carried out.

- Cost over-runs can become a problem area when control measures are not taken.
- Programme adherence if the goals are not shared with the team. If these are visible for all to see then members will better work together to help others meet their deadlines.
- Team members not knowing what areas they are responsible for and who is accountable for them.
- The team being diverted from the main project tasks and trying to fit other things in which could be postponed to a more opportune time.

Where conflict does occur it may be seen in a whole range of behaviours such as:

- Tears, raised voices, aggressive horseplay, even physical fights!
- Statements expressing negative feelings – jealousy, distrust, derision, fear, dislike – about a group or individual.
- Individuals being prevented from getting the rewards that are normally given to people who have performed as well as they have.
- People choosing not to pass on useful information to others.

- Individuals refusing to talk to one another – or doing so only with, say, icy formality, sarcastic remarks or open aggression.
- People setting up barriers – being unavailable or approachable only through their own private rules and procedures.
- People being off "sick" or otherwise absent more frequently than seems normal.
- Low morale and poor productivity especially if the people concerned blame others.

When conflict does occur there are three options open to move forward; the first is to ignore it and assume that it will sort it self out (this may be termed "non-intervention"); the second is to prevent it occurring by taking early action ("preventive strategy"); and the third is to resolve the problem (this may be termed "resolution"). In trying to resolve conflict, five methods are suggested: direct approach, bargaining, enforcement, retreat and de-emphasis. These are detailed below as each can be used effectively depending on the circumstances of the conflict.

- The **direct approach** may be the best option as it concentrates on the leader confronting the issue head-on. Though conflict is for many unpleasant to deal with, if criticism is used then it must be constructive to the recipients. This approach draws on the techniques of problem solving and because issues are brought to the surface and dealt with it normally ends with mutual resolution.

- **Bargaining** is an excellent technique applicable when both parties have ideas on a solution yet cannot find common ground. Often the team leader can use this to find a compromise solution. On the other hand, as it requires both sides to reach agreement, there is a risk that it can also result in both parties feeling equally dissatisfied.
- **Enforcement** of team rules is an option to be avoided if possible as it can bring about hard feelings towards the leader and the team. This technique is best used when it is obvious that a member does not want to be a team player and refuses to work with the rest.
- **Retreat** is an option when the problem is not real to start with and delay in addressing it can allow the individual to cool off.
- **De-emphasis** is a form of bargaining where the focus is on the areas of agreement so that the parties realize that there are areas of agreement which can then be used to work on addressing the minor differences.

Team conflict should first be handled on an informal basis between the individuals involved. This should allow time for resolution or self-correction by the individuals. The team leader may act as the mediator or even as advocate, and if resolution is still not achieved the dispute should be openly discussed in a team meeting. If the team are still unable to agree their differences and work together a formal discipline process will need to be used.

Because every team is different, disputes that arise will be too, so in order to resolve their differences, Varney's 1989 book on building productive teams recommends bringing the parties together and, with the assistance of a third party, asking the following five questions:

1. What is the problem, as you perceive it?
2. What does the other person do that contributes to the problem?
3. What do you want or need from the other person?
4. What do you do that contributes to the problem?
5. What first step can you take to resolve the problem?

In this technique each party is questioned while the other listens and is only permitted to ask questions for clarification. The parties then discuss a mutual definition and understanding of the problem. Whilst they are allowed to express their feelings and get hostility out of their systems at this stage, it is important that both parties admit partial responsibility for the problem. This requires the team leader to have good listening skills and the ability to stay in a problem-solving mode. Agreement can then be reached on what steps need to be taken to resolve the problem; to prevent later misunderstandings these should be put in writing.

The professional management of people using knowledge, skills and hopefully the tools and guidance notes of this chapter is an important part of transforming business plans and strategic aspirations into reality through the willing engagement of people in various roles such as product development, marketing, supply chain working and in-house tasks and teamworking. On this basis people management is clearly a key aspect of operations management whether in the provision of goods or services. In this final chapter on people it is again worth noting that this is an area which contributes to the topic of operations management as shown in Figure 1.2 and offers a tactical operational focus illustrated in the book's Introduction.

REFERENCES

Adair, J. (1988) *Effective Leadership*. Pan Publishing, London.

Ansoff, H.I. (1957) Strategies for diversification. *Harvard Business Review*, September–October 1957, Volume 35, Number 5.

Barksdale, H.C. and Harris, C.E. (1982) Portfolio analysis and the product life cycle. *Journal of Long Range Planning*, pages 74–93, Number 15. Elsevier Publishing.

Belbin, R.M. (2004) *Management Teams: Why They Succeed or Fail*. Butterworth Heinemann, 2nd edition. ISBN 0750659106.

British Standards Institute. BS 25999-2:2007 *Business Continuity Management*. Published November 2007. ISBN 9780580599132.1

Burtonshaw-Gunn, S.A. (2004) Examining risk and supply chain collaborative working, in *Supply Chain Risk*. Editor Professor C.S. Brindley. Ashgate Publishing, UK. ISBN 9780754639022.

Burtonshaw-Gunn, S.A. and Salameh, M.G. (2007) *The Role of Strategic Executive Development*. ICAFI University Press, Hyderabad, India. October 2007.

Burtonshaw-Gunn, S.A. (2008) *The Essential Management Toolbox: Models, Tools and Notes for Managers and Consultants*. John Wiley and Sons, UK. ISBN 97800470518373.

Burtonshaw-Gunn, S.A. and Salameh, M.G. (2009) *Essential Tools for Organizational Performance: Models, Tools and Notes for Managers and Consultants.* John Wiley and Sons, UK. ISBN 9780470746653.

Burtonshaw-Gunn, S.A. (2010) *Essential Tools for Management Consulting: Models, Tools and Notes for Managers and Consultants.* John Wiley and Sons, UK. ISBN 9780470745939.2

Cox, A. (1999) Power, value and supply chain management. *Supply Chain Management*, Volume 4, Issue 4, pages 167–175.

"Innovation in Industry" survey, *The Economist*, 20th February 1999.

Johnson, G. and Scholes, K. (2002) *Exploring Corporate Strategy.* Pearson Education, 6th edition.

Lock, D. (ed.) (1992) *The Handbook of Management*, 3rd edition. Gower Publishing Limited. ISBN 9780566029745.

Sadgrove, K. (1994) *The Green Guide to Profitable Management.* Gower Publications. ISBN 9780566075421.

Tuckman, B.W. and Jenson, M.A.C. (1977) Development sequences in small groups. *Psychological Bulletin*, Volume 63, Number 6. The American Psychological Association.

Varney, G.H. (1989) *Building Productive Teams: An Action Guide and Resource Book.* Jossey-Bass Inc., San Francisco, CA.

INDEX

Index compiled by Annette Musker